D1188306

THOMAS JEFFERSON
Philosopher and President

THOMAS JEFFERSON
Philosopher and President

Nancy Whitelaw

MORGAN
REYNOLDS
Publishers, Inc.

620 South Elm Street, Suite 223
Greensboro, North Carolina   27406
http://www.morganreynolds.com

THOMAS JEFFERSON: PHILOSOPHER AND PRESIDENT

Library of Congress Cataloging-in-Publication Data

Whitelaw, Nancy
    Thomas Jefferson : philosopher and president / Nancy Whitelaw.
       p. cm.
    Includes bibliographical references and index.
    Summary: An account of Jefferson's life highlighting his many accomplishments as
governor, architect, gardener, inventor, and president.
    ISBN 1-883846-81-1
       1. Jefferson, Thomas, 1743-1826--Juvenile literature. 2. Presidents--United
States--Biography--Juvenile literature. [1. Jefferson, Thomas, 1743-1826. 2. Presidents.]
I. Title.

E332.79 .W47 2001
973.4'6'092--dc21
[B]
                                                                        2001044960

Printed in the United States of America
First Edition

Dedicated to Laura Renker with admiration and appreciation for her fine work, enthusiasm, and support for volunteers at the Dispute Settlement Centers of Chautauqua County in western New York.

Contents

Thomas Jefferson
(Courtesy of the Library of Congress)

Chapter One

The Young Jefferson

Thomas Jefferson was born in 1743 on the edge of the wilderness in the colony of Virginia. At that time, about one and a half million colonists lived in British America, and the population was growing rapidly.

Tom's father, Peter, brought up his children in the unspoiled land of Virginia, a place that left young Tom with a love of the land throughout his life. Peter Jefferson enjoyed social status and wealth in his estate at Shadwell, which he had named for the parish in England where his wife, Jane Randolph Jefferson, was born. Peter was an ambitious farmer, surveyor, and map maker. Like all wealthy farmers in Virginia, he had slaves to do most of the work. Peter Jefferson was also a justice of the peace and a member of the House of Burgesses, the colonial Virginia legislature.

The Jeffersons had a home library of books and maps, which was supplemented with books from the nearby Tuckahoe Library. Some stories say that Tom read all his father's books before he was five years old, including the Bible and a history of England. In the evenings when he was home, Peter taught his son his love of mathematics and books, penmanship, and an appreciation of nature.

At five years old, Tom began his education. Everyday, he and some male cousins were sent to a small building in the yard of the Jefferson home where they studied with a tutor. Tom often ended his morning prayer with a plea to be excused from school. He could not understand why it seemed that his black slave playmates were so much luckier than he was. Because they were not allowed to go to school, slave children were free to romp in the fields and forests until their masters had chores for them.

While Tom was still young, his father expanded his plain Virginia farmhouse into a spacious country house. Tom grew up with construction projects all around him. It was at Shadwell that he first began dreaming of building his own home.

At nine, Tom was sent away to a boarding school, where he studied French, Latin, and Greek. To Tom, the best thing about boarding school was coming home on vacations. He spent each summer at Shadwell, often riding alone in the area around his home. The Jefferson family, which then included eight children, spent evenings around the fireplace together. Tom's older sister Jane encouraged him to learn to read music, and Peter gave him a violin that Tom learned to play and love. Whenever Tom's father was home, the two spent time

These sketches from 1740 show public buildings of Williamsburg, the capital of the Virginia colony. Peter Jefferson was a delegate to the House of Burgesses which met in the capitol, pictured on the lower left (#4). *(Courtesy of the Library of Congress)*

together, riding, paddling a canoe on the Rivanna River, talking about nature, and always enjoying the outdoors. Peter Jefferson also taught his son about surveying and map making.

Making maps fascinated Tom. Knowledge of boundaries and frontiers was essential to the colonists who were establishing homes and businesses in this mostly unexplored land. Early in the history of colonization of the New World, boundaries were created and questioned by three nations—Britain, France, and Spain. European leaders wanted to define and extend their territories, although they were unsure about what they could expect to gain from the colonies. The rumors about gold and silver tempted some, but land, opportunities for commerce, and other natural resources were more definite gains. In any case, leaders of each of the three countries were ready to fight for the chance to expand their holdings in the American wilderness.

By the mid 1700s, New France included land stretching north of what is now Quebec, across the Great Lakes, and through the Louisiana Territory that reached the Gulf of Mexico at New Orleans. New Spain stretched from what is now eastern Texas westward to the Pacific Ocean and south to what is now Honduras. It also included Florida and Cuba. The English claims were divided into two geographic areas. One was a large region around the Hudson Bay, and the other was the eastern seaboard from what is now Boston, Massachusetts, to Charleston, South Carolina.

Conflict between the French and British colonies exploded into warfare in 1754 when Tom was about twelve years old. The French and Indian War began when British settlers moved westward from the colony of Virginia to the Ohio Territory, land which the French claimed. The Iroquois Indians entered the conflict on the side of the French. Fearing that Native Americans might someday unite against British settlers, representatives of the colonies of New Hampshire, Massachusetts, Connecticut, Rhode Island, Pennsylvania, Maryland, and New York met in Albany to solidify their relationship with the native people. This group created the Albany Plan of Union to unite the seven colonies under a single government. But when the representatives returned to their colonial governments with the

King George III ascended the English throne in 1760. *(Courtesy of the Library of Congress)*

plan, each colony rejected it, saying it called for too strong a central government.

When Tom was fourteen years old, his father died. Tom found nothing or no one to ease his grief. He wrote that he felt "thrown on a wide world, among entire strangers, without a friend or guardian to advise." He gained no comfort from his mother or siblings.

Peter left instructions for Tom to continue his education. So once again he left home to board at school during the week. Reverend James Maury, headmaster of a log schoolhouse, owned a library even bigger than Tom's father's. Tom read many of the 400 books, learned Greek and Latin, and studied history and mythology. He became fascinated with the causes of the rise and fall of the Roman Empire and the leaders who hastened it: ambitious Gaius Julius Caesar; vengeful Catiline; and lenient Hadrian, who believed that governments and armies should exist for the welfare of the state. He was fascinated by stories of civil rebellions, struggles for power within government, conflicts between political and military groups, assassination attempts, and military and political strategies. Tom read fiction and plays as well. He wrote to a friend that in reading Shakespeare, Moliere, Addison, and others, "lessons may be formed to illustrate and carry home to the heart every moral rule of life."

At age sixteen, Tom was tall and slim, with chestnut hair and lots of freckles. His enthusiasm for life showed in everything he did—he loved the outdoors, reading, riding, dancing, and playing his fiddle. On weekends at Shadwell, he often explored the countryside on horseback. He read Greek, Latin, and French literature in the original language.

Not content with simply reading, Tom kept an annotated record of much of what he learned and thought. In a kind of journal that he called a commonplace book, he kept notes on his reading, sometimes paraphrasing, sometimes summarizing, sometimes copying, and usually adding his own thoughts. He even wrote some of these pages in Greek and Latin.

One well-known anecdote about Tom's love of learning begins that Tom wrote to John Harvie, a family friend who was guardian of Tom's inheritance. Tom complained to Harvie that there was too much socializ-

ing at Shadwell during the weekends, making it difficult for him to pursue his studies. Tom proposed that he
attend William and Mary College in Williamsburg. Harvie
allowed him to enroll in the spring of 1760.

Chapter Two

College Years

When seventeen-year-old Tom left Shadwell for William and Mary, he took books, his fiddle, and Jupiter, his slave who was his same age. (It was not uncommon for young men of means to have a slave accompany them to college.) He also took a brilliant mind, intellectual curiosity, and a strong background in the classics and in history. He had a tendency towards shyness. One friend said, "His manners could never be harsh, but they were reserved towards the world at large." Tom had no specific career goals at that time.

Williamsburg looked very sophisticated to Tom. A thousand people lived in the Virginia capital. At one end of a mile-long street was the governor's large house, and at the other end stood the three brick buildings of the college. All along the street, which was wide enough for several carriages to drive side by side, were houses and shops. The shops dazzled Tom, who had never seen clothes of silk and damask, satin and velvet.

During his first year, Tom felt he spent too much

time horse racing and fox hunting, so as he began his second year at William and Mary, he wrote an apology to Harvie. "Which of these kinds of reputation should I prefer? That of a horse jockey? Or a fox hunter? An orator? Or the honest advocate of my country's rights?" he admonished himself. He suggested that the cost of his first year be subtracted from his inheritance because he had worked so little. Harvie said this was unnecessary, and he understood that Tom had learned an important lesson. Tom kept his promise to work hard and found that he did not have to give up all the social aspects of his life.

Math was one of Tom's favorite subjects; he carried a ruler and a book of logarithms (algebraic equations) wherever he went. He worked hard to become a model of self-improvement. He was not pushed to make a career choice. As the son of an aristocrat, he had three socially acceptable choices—to continue his father's farming, become a member of the clergy, or become a lawyer. No matter which path he chose, Tom hoped to be able to continue his studies for the rest of his life.

Later he wrote that his teacher Dr. William Small "fixed the destinies of my life." Dr. Small taught mathematics, rhetoric, science, and ethics. Both student and professor enjoyed each other's company. Dr. Small often invited young Tom to join him at dinner with the acting attorney for the colony of Virginia, George Wythe, and Royal Governor Francis Fauquier. These older men became Tom's role models.

Tom was particularly interested in their discussions of the rise and fall of the Roman Empire. As a mighty civilization, the Romans created a government with many democratic principles and a respect for the rights of most men. Their development of arts and sciences was dazzling as well. But the Roman Republic did not last; it devolved into a dictatorship controlled by often corrupt rulers characterized by greed, self-indulgence, obsession with power, and a decline of morals. When Roman leaders began to seek personal gain, the republic was destroyed. These ideas influenced Tom throughout his life.

Some of Tom's opinions evolved from his early life among frontiersmen. Unaffected by the community of commerce that developed in urban areas, frontier people insisted on their basic rights rather than on rights associated with property or privilege. They were also more willing to take risks in hopes of bettering their lives than people in the older settlements whose lives were more comfortable. Tom began to believe that an individual required little or no external discipline, such as laws and strong governments, to live productively and happily in his community.

To defend his beliefs to his friends, Tom used the example of the Saxons of England. In his journal, or commonplace book, Tom wrote that in the fifth century, the Saxons had lived under natural law in England without government restrictions. They had lost this freedom when government and religious officials vying for authority diminished individual rights. Most of his fellow students and professors saw this as a simplified version of history. They scoffed that only in a fantasy world could an individual live in a community without civil laws and the threat of punishments.

Living in cosmopolitan Williamsburg, Tom was aware of the tension developing between England and the colonies. Tom's interest in law and government grew as the conflicts increased. He read the works of great writers of the eighteenth-century Enlightenment, the period in Europe and America that was marked by strong faith in the power of human reason. These philosophers sought the discovery of truth through observation rather than through the acceptance of earlier authority, such as that in organized religion. They focused on worldly happiness above religious salvation in the next life. Tom paid special attention to what John Locke called the "natural law." This law attacked the divine right of kings to rule and supported the right of citizens to rebel against government. Tom saw this idea reflected in Virginia's House of Burgesses. Although few other colonies had their own legislative body, the Burgesses was establishing its role in the shadow of the authority of the British crown and Parliament.

At the age of nineteen, Tom decided to take up the study of law after graduating from William and Mary in 1762. There were no law schools, so he followed the accepted practice of studying under an established attorney. George Wythe, a man for whom Tom had developed deep respect while at college, agreed to be his tutor. Wythe's attitude toward law fit perfectly into Tom's instincts and background. Wythe believed that law was a science, and his new student eagerly grasped scientific methods. Along with being a student, Tom was also an intern who was expected to conduct legal research and to follow closely each step that his master took in court.

An eager student, Tom read the material Wythe suggested by British jurists, and he continued to read Greek, Latin, French, and English literature as well as many books about philosophy. He spent more time in his study of law than he had in all his other studies as a college student. He often worked from 5 a.m. through the evening, taking time off only for a jog through the countryside each afternoon. He carefully scheduled his reading to fit into what he considered the most appropriate times of day. Each morning he spent the first three hours of study on ethics and religion. Then he moved into legal studies. After lunch he read politics, then he read history—mostly Greek and Roman but also some European—and he also read the classics, such as Homer's *The Iliad* and *The Odyssey*, and the Roman poet Virgil. To young Tom, the classics were more than a luxury. They were his masters and counselors. They revealed to him the great problems of life and of human conduct. Most of the people he knew did not share this faith in the classics. Virginia was a land of very strong Church of England traditions, and it was expected that one could receive all the moral training one needed by studying the Bible. In the evening, Tom wrote letters in his commonplace books, reviewed his reading, and practiced rhetoric.

In his commonplace books, he began to note historical examples of colonies refusing to be subjected to their mother countries. Already thinking like a lawyer, he began tracing a line of precedents. He studied constitutions and histories to determine what made a country strong and what weakened it. Tom also took great interest in studying the laws and religious practices of Britain, comparing these with the way other countries formed their laws and religious practices. Each of these particular subjects helped Tom to become a more effective lawyer. He wrote, "a lawyer without books would be like a workman without tools." Throughout all his studies, he focused on the logic of the 'natural' world, believing that with reason a man can find self-evident truths that are both permanent and universal.

As he progressed in his studies, Tom spent more time in the General Court of Virginia, where cases concerning land holdings, felonies, and such issues were heard. Here his study of law shifted from the theoretical to the practical. He applied for admission to the elite bar of the Virginia General Court in Williamsburg, was accepted, and soon became known for his meticulous presentation of both civil and criminal cases. Without fear, Tom attacked what he considered to be injustice, whether the source was a common man or a federal judge. He was especially known for his skill in land ownership cases, a growing issue given the colonies' continually expanding frontiers.

In the course of his investigations of cases concerning land ownership, Jefferson bought and sold land for himself. He doubled both the amount of land he owned and his profit from tobacco crops. As he traveled, he kept detailed accounts of his experiences. He often wrote poetically: "Descending, then, to the valley below, the sensation becomes delightful in the extreme . . . It is impossible for the emotions, arising from the sublime, to be felt beyond what they are here."

Jefferson's studies in law consolidated ideas that had been building in his mind for several years and set the stage for his political ambitions. He believed that part of a legal education should include time spent in the legislature, so he visited the House of Burgesses. It was expected that a man of his social status and education would at some time be a member of the House of Burgesses, and Tom was preparing to take his turn. While observing, he was fascinated by the explosive speeches of representative Patrick Henry, who had studied law around the same time as Tom. Henry favored breaking away from British rule, and he saw it as his mission to persuade other Burgesses to agree with him. Tom never forgot the scene when a member of the Burgesses interrupted Henry's speech with shouts of "Treason! Treason." Henry calmly answered the heckler: "If this be treason, make the most of it!"

Although he sometimes differed with Patrick Henry about politics, Jefferson found his passionate speeches inspiring. *(Courtesy of the Library of Congress)*

Tom watched closely the power struggle developing between Britain and the American colonies. Crises, small and large, developed as the British and the colonists vied for control. The British won vast new territories when the French and Indian War ended in 1763, and with the land they also gained new problems. One problem was how to deal with the Native Americans who had shown allegiance to France, but who lived on land now claimed by Britain. Another problem was protection of the colonial settlers who wanted to move into the newly-acquired land. Still a third problem was the staggering debt left by the war. Over the next few years, these problems, and the efforts Britain made to deal with them, drove a wedge between the home country and the colonies.

The crown attempted to deal with land squabbles by securing the western lands captured from the French. They set up a boundary line on the eastern side of the Appalachian Mountains that no settlers would be allowed to move west of. With this boundary, they hoped to keep the revenue from land and fur speculation in British hands and to control the colonists by limiting their movement. The crown also claimed that the colonies owed them a debt because British soldiers had fought to protect colonial land in the French and Indian War. To collect this debt, they imposed a number of taxes on goods imported from England. Until this time, British taxes were imposed in the name of regulating trade, never to raise revenue for the British government. The Sugar Act of 1764 levied new duties on indigo, coffee, wine, cloth, and sugar. This enraged many of the colonists, who declared that the British Parliament had no right to collect taxes from citizens to fill the coffers of the crown. The call of "no taxation without representation" was heard more and more often.

The passage of three more acts further enraged the colonists. The Currency Act of 1764 demanded that the colonists stop issuing their own currency. Then the crown announced that the next year they would impose a Stamp Act, which would levy a duty on all printed documents, including almanacs, newspapers, and pamphlets. Finally, the Quartering Act of 1765 required colonists to provide British soldiers with room and board. The announcement of these acts ignited storms of protest in the colonies.

Chapter Three

Political Beginnings

Tom followed the news of the developing tensions between the colonies and the crown eagerly, although he was not yet ready to take sides. In 1766, he was admitted to the General Court bar, making him eligible to work on both civil and criminal cases.

That same year, King George III of England decreed that the colonists would have to increase their payments to the mother country, and Parliament imposed more taxes. Chancellor of the Exchequer, Charles Townshend, proposed new taxes that came to be called the Townshend Acts, which levied an import tax on glass, white lead, paper, and tea. The colonists objected, especially to the tax on tea, a drink enjoyed by a million colonists twice a day. Parliament added what at first seemed like a bonus: The colonists would no longer have to pay the salaries of their judges and governors; now England would assume the payments. The colonists soon recognized this "bonus" for what it was—a plan to impose British control over these important officials.

Tom was now convinced that the acts of the crown were unfair to the colonists. Representative Patrick Henry exploded in a legislative meeting of the Burgesses, shouting "Parliament has enslaved us!" Tom admired the fiery style of his friend, but he could not emulate Henry's passionate way of speaking. His voice became strained after just a few moments of public speaking. However, his shyness did not prevent him from believing as forcefully as Henry did.

Citizens of other colonies joined the protest. The Massachusetts legislature reacted to the news of the Townshend Acts with a "circular letter," so-called because the message was sent around to each of the colonies. In this letter, Massachusetts declared that it would resist the taxes by every legal means and urged the other colonies to do the same. This circular letter both united and divided the colonists. Some were increasingly ready to fight against the authority of the crown. Others became more determined to defend the crown and to remain loyal to Great Britain.

The Townshend Acts were an important factor in Tom's decision to run for representative to the House of Burgesses. His training told him that precedent was all-important. He noted that after the Saxons emigrated from Denmark to England, Denmark claimed no authority over these emigrants. In the same progression of thought, he declared, England should claim no authority over the immigrants who came to America. Beyond all these reasons, his role in the Burgesses would fulfill one of his obligations as a member of the aristocracy.

In 1768, Tom began to build a house on a hilltop near his mother's home. At first, he planned a small home with just one guest room. He declared that he intended to live simply like the ancient Spartans. Before the house was finished, politics took his attention from this project. He spent several months campaigning for the Burgesses seat that had been his father's. He won the election due to his fine reputation as a lawyer who won most of his cases, and also his many acquaintances.

In the spring of 1769, Representative Jefferson took up his legislative duties. To the young lawyer it seemed to be an awesome responsibility. In his autobiography he wrote, "Our minds were circumscribed within narrow limits by an habitual belief that it was our duty to be subordinate to the mother country in all matters of government."

His first assignment was to write a formal reply to an address by Virginia Governor Baron de Botetourt. The governor had warned the representatives to think carefully about the interests of those whom they represented. Jefferson began his address traditionally, affirming the loyalty of the colonists to the crown. He declared that the interests of the crown and the Burgesses were the same. He went on to point out that there were differences—very large differences—in the ways Parliament and the Burgesses saw their roles and responsibilities to the colonists. Mincing no words, Jefferson declared that the rights of the colonists had been violated by unfair acts and taxation. Before sending the message to the king, Jefferson had to read it to the representatives for their approval.

Heads were shaking before Jefferson finished the first few paragraphs. Representatives told him that his message was too close in meaning to resolutions already submitted to British authorities. They said his ideas needed more elaboration. They picked his draft apart, editing, deleting, and enlarging it. Jefferson felt angry and humiliated. For the next several meetings, he spoke little, if at all.

Although the representatives spent hours working on the reply, Botetourt took only a few minutes to respond. Immediately after reading it, the governor summoned the representatives to his council chamber. In April 1769, he told them, "You have made it my duty to dissolve you and you are dissolved accordingly."

The representatives reacted swiftly. They moved to the Apollo Room of the nearby Raleigh Tavern and continued with their business. In their anger, they were stronger and more united than before. One of their first acts was to sign the Non-importation Resolution, an agreement to boycott all British goods, even the most popular, such as tea, wine, meat, clothing material, and oil. They would lift the boycott, they said, when Britain removed duties from imports. Even more resolute after making that declaration, they vowed that a British attack on one colony was an attack on all colonies.

Jefferson signed the resolution. As he wrote in his

commonplace book, he advocated a strong union of colonies because "mutual defense against a more powerful neighbor is in early times the chief, or sole motive for joining society."

Although busy with government, Jefferson took time to work on planning his house, but during the planning, his original idea for a small and simple home faded away. He became interested in architecture while studying history at William and Mary, and now he wanted to put those studies to good use. He knew where he wanted to build—on top of the mountain near Shadwell. His site on the edge of the wilderness offered a panoramic view of the Blue Ridge Mountains. Friends and relatives laughed at him and said that he should build on level ground. In rebuttal, Jefferson named his estate *Monticello*, Italian for "low mountain." Some saw his choice of an isolated site away from the community as a reflection of his shyness.

Tom resolved to be both architect and builder on the project to the extent that time would allow. The immense project began with clearing and leveling the summit. Transporting building supplies and water to the site posed a huge challenge. When he began the project in 1768, the same year that he was elected to legislature, Tom could not have guessed that his desire for perfection would push him to plan, create, revise, enlarge, and renovate for forty years, long after he had moved in.

In July 1769, the first 45,000 bricks were delivered,

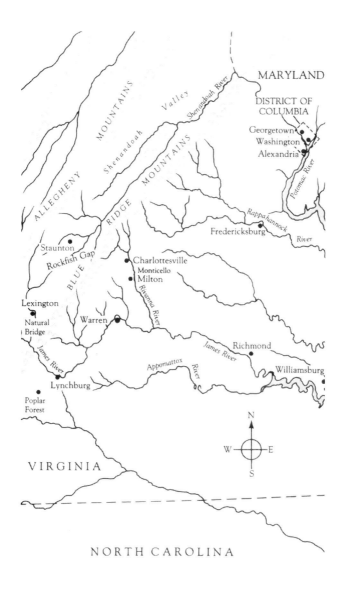

and a path was cleared around the site. He planted fruit trees—pear, cherry, apple, apricot, nectarine, fig, and peach—and recorded details of plantings and growth in his garden book.

Jefferson studied the books of Italian architect Andrea Palladio, who wrote about Roman architecture in 1570. He gave the workmen engravings of Palladio's buildings and wrote on them the dimensions he wanted for his two-story house. He researched the building of his home as he would have researched a legal case, with specific details in every step of the process. In October, he moved into a small brick cottage on the grounds of Monticello. For the next two years, Jefferson lived in the cottage while he worked on his home and continued his studies of law, government, and history.

His goal with Monticello was to create a home where he could live an idyllic life. As the Roman poet Horace wrote: "Happy the man who, far away from business cares, works his ancestral acres with his steers, from all money-lending free; he avoids the Forum and proud thresholds of more powerful citizens."

But the Burgesses and public life called to Jefferson again in the late summer of 1771. Busy with problems caused by the worst flood in Virginia's history, the Burgesses scarcely paid attention to the news from Massachusetts about what people called the Boston Massacre, where British soldiers had killed three civilians in the street.

A Committee of Safety had been appointed to enforce the Non-importation Acts, forbidding Virginians to import tea, paper, or glass, when Jefferson's order of fourteen windows arrived from Europe. His home was so important to him that although he had helped draft the acts, he appealed to his political friends to grant him an exception to this rule. The Committee of Safety released the windows to him.

Jefferson was not the only Virginian who received imported goods. Some citizens who were loyal to the British paid whatever taxes were imposed without complaining. However, thousands of citizens and slaves remained outside the conflict, unable to afford imports anyway.

All over Virginia there were citizens who clung to their British traditions, heritage, and loyalties, and there were citizens who eagerly sought to define themselves as creators of American independence. Families were split with some members eager to fight for the Patriot cause, while others were appalled at any thought of rebellion.

Women in Virginia were divided in their reactions to the fiery representatives in the House of Burgesses. Wealthy women loyal to Britain carried on their social life as usual, flaunting their ability to smuggle in European clothes, tea, and other imports. Many Patriot women were just as proud of their determination to obey the acts: to wear homespun and simple clothes, to concoct substitute drinks for tea, and to brag that they supported the idea for independence for the colonies. Still other Patriot women were bewildered and afraid to stand up for either side.

Along with fulfilling his dream of building the perfect house, Jefferson also fulfilled another dream—that of a happy marriage and family. He had been courting a young widow, twenty-four-year-old Martha Skelton, for over two years. Martha was tall and had lovely auburn hair. She loved to read, especially novels, and shared with Tom an appreciation and talent for music. There is a story that two other suitors called on Martha and sat on the terrace while she and Jefferson played a duet on harpsichord and violin inside the parlor. Listening to the two harmonize, the two men supposedly left without being announced. They saw no point in staying. Martha brought a three-year-old son to the marriage and the next fall, she gave birth to a daughter. Although the couple named their daughter Martha, they chose to call her "Patsy."

In March 1773, Jefferson met with Patrick Henry, Richard Henry Lee, and Francis Lightfoot Lee to discuss the failure of the non-importation movement. The British did not seem to notice a loss in tax revenue, and Patriot businessmen felt overburdened by the import restrictions. The four men drew up a list of resolutions for Governor Botetourt's replacement, Governor John Dunmore. They informed Dunmore that the Burgesses would not allow Parliament to dominate their trade and commerce.

Jefferson was elected to head the Albemarle County

Committee of Safety and also to represent the county in the upcoming first Virginia Convention, a group that was organized to elect a delegation to send to the First Continental Congress.

In the summer of 1774, Jefferson started off for the convention with his paper called "Draft of Instructions to the Virginia Delegates in the Continental Congress." The Continental Congress was a group of representatives that would be selected from each colony to meet in Philadelphia in September 1774. These representatives would attempt to unify the colonies under common policies and discuss new resolutions and forms of protest. They were not, however, intended to act as an insurgent governing body.

Jefferson's "Instructions to the Virginia Delegates," his most rebellious writing yet, cut straight to the question of the crown's authority. In his paper, Jefferson declared that the colonies were not subject to any laws or taxes except those imposed by their own colonial legislatures. He stated that the colonists had earned the right to freedom by their sacrifice to build their own settlements. Jefferson outlined the specific abuses of the king: neglecting the colonists, dissolving colonial assemblies, refusing to hear appeals, delaying the passage of land reforms, sending armed troops into American cities, prohibiting westward migration of settlers, and perpetuating slavery by blocking colonial efforts to end the practice. At times, Jefferson's language sounded more like commands than pleas: "Open your breast, Sire, to liberal and expanded thought. Let not the name of George the third be a blot in the page of history." The draft concludes with the famous phrase, "The God who gave us life gave us liberty at the same time." Unfortunately, on the way to Williamsburg, Jefferson became ill and had to turn back, and his fellow delegates presented the draft for him.

Reactions to "Instructions to the Virginia Delegates" were mixed. Most of the older representatives rejected it completely. They wanted to know how a few colonies, isolated from each other and without any central authority, hoped to challenge the strongest country in the world. Some of the younger representatives applauded loudly and enthusiastically, sure that the justness of their cause would lead them to victory.

After much discussion, the representatives did not pass the resolutions Jefferson asked for, nor was Jefferson selected to be a delegate to the First Continental Congress. Some of his supporters did have the draft reprinted and distributed as "A Summary View of the Rights of British America." With publication of this pamphlet, Jefferson became known as a leading radical. Members of the British Parliament labeled him an outlaw.

Chapter Four

Declaration of Independence

Jefferson became a delegate to the second Virginia Convention in Williamsburg in 1775. The convention was held to discuss how Virginia should react to Great Britain and how it should cooperate with the other colonies. At this meeting, Patrick Henry spoke very forcefully for open conflict against Great Britain. His speech ended with the now famous phrase, "Give me liberty or give me death." Henry once again proved that he was one of the strongest and most dramatic speakers of the day. Jefferson was torn between his desire to make his opinion known and his fear of speaking after such a fine orator. He was well aware that his voice was soft and hoarse, but he could not resist the opportunity to display his thoughts, and he seconded Henry's ideas enthusiastically. The resolution calling for an American militia passed by sixty-five to sixty votes. Jefferson was appointed to prepare a plan for training and arming soldiers. At the end of the convention, Jefferson was selected as alternate to the Second Continental Congress, which would convene in Philadelphia in May 1775.

In the months preceding the Continental Congress, the creation of his dream home at Monticello called to Jefferson as loudly as the conflicts of government. He was delighted with his home and grounds. He continued to record the events of his garden in his garden book, including temperature and rainfall. He also kept a ledger recording all his expenses, from the most trivial to the biggest.

Although reluctant to be away from Monticello, in June 1775 Jefferson accepted a call to replace an absent representative at the Second Continental Congress. He departed, aware that he was headed straight for the eye of a storm. Most of the representatives had already decided to make the break from the mother country, and Jefferson knew this meant war. King George III had declared that "blows must decide whether they [the colonies] are to be subject to the Country or Independent." Direct and open gun battles had occurred that spring in Lexington and Concord in Massachusetts. A few days later the bloody battles of Bunker Hill and Breed's Hill had proven to the British that the patriot forces were not going to surrender at the first sight of the British troops in their bright red uniforms with guns, bayonets, and swords.

Security was tight when the delegates met in the Pennsylvania State House in Philadelphia. Representatives locked the doors and would open the windows a

The Continental Congress met at the Philadelphia State House, which was later renamed Independence Hall. *(Courtesy of the Library of Congress)*

mere crack in spite of the muggy weather. Jefferson met old friends and made new acquaintances. Among the old friends was General George Washington, recently appointed commander-in-chief of the Continental Army, in his elegant uniform with gold epaulets and a sword at his side. New friends included John and Samuel Adams and John Hancock from Boston, and Benjamin Franklin from Pennsylvania.

John Adams became a good friend, although at first glance it would seem that the two men could not have been more different. Jefferson hardly spoke a word in the meetings; Adams let few topics go by without his opinion. Jefferson spent lavishly on books, clothes, and anything that struck his fancy. Adams bought nothing but the necessities. Jefferson kept meticulous and detailed accounts of purchases, readings, daily temperature, and comments on the physical world around him. Adams kept rambling notes about people he met and his reactions to them. Adams was eight years older than Jefferson. Jefferson was over six feet tall, slim, and had a head of thick, coppery hair. Adams was short and stout and balding. But both men shared a love of learning, a deep knowledge of the classics, and, most importantly, a dream of an independent America.

Jefferson worked with other delegates to write "A Declaration on the Necessity of Taking Up Arms." He was unhappy with the final draft because, as usual, the other committee members edited his writing. This paper sent several strong messages to the crown. The representatives declared that Parliament had no right to dissolve a colonial legislature and that the colonies did not need or want Parliament to make laws for them. Parliament and the king received written notice that the colonies believed they were strong enough to be victorious if the conflict should escalate to war.

After the Congress recessed for the summer, Jefferson returned to spend a few days in Williamsburg, where he was elected to return to the Congress when it re-convened in September. He was then free to return to the family he missed so much—Martha, Patsy, and his

John Adams was Jefferson's opposite in many ways, but both men shared a deep commitment to the patriot cause. *(Courtesy of the Library of Congress)*

second daughter Jane, who was born in March 1774. Just as Jefferson was preparing to leave Monticello again for Philadelphia in early September, seventeen-month-old Jane died. Jefferson saw that Martha was with her sister before he left.

In July, Pennsylvania congressional Representative John Dickinson had written a message to King George expressing allegiance to the crown and begging him to stop all hostile action until mediation could ease the conflict. Dickinson's Olive Branch Petition was approved by Congress and sent on to London. Jefferson did not expect it to meet with the king's approval. Word of George III's refusal to consider the request arrived in November. The king insisted that the colonists put down their guns and submit to the will of the crown in all issues. Among the representatives, there was disagreement about how to react to the king's missive. Some representatives interpreted the king's refusal to negoti-

A copy of Dickinson's Olive Branch Petition, July 5, 1775.

ate as a declaration of war. Others clung to their allegiance to Britain, arguing that they needed the crown to pursue their lives and businesses, and that it was nothing short of treason to continue the armed rebellion. It soon became clear that the Patriots were in the majority, though, and the members of the Congress began the task of preparing for war—raising money, enlisting soldiers, starting a navy, and appeasing the Native Americans who might stand against them.

Jefferson's own patience with the crown was at an end. "Can any reason be assigned why 160,000 electors in the island of Great Britain should give law to four million in the states of America, every individual of whom is equal to every individual of them in virtue, in understanding, and in bodily strength?" Jefferson asked. He wrote to a cousin in England that "we must drub you soundly before the sceptered tyrant will know we are not mere brutes, to crouch under his hand and kiss the rod with which he deigns to scourge us."

Jefferson left Philadelphia for the Christmas holiday. As he traveled to Virginia, he heard the news that Virginia Governor Dunmore had established martial law in Norfolk and had ordered all residents to take up arms for the British or to leave the colony. Dunmore offered freedom to any slave who would flee his master to fight for the king. Three hundred slaves accepted the offer. The king's troops bombarded the city, leaving only about one-fifth of the buildings standing.

At Monticello, Martha was frail and sickly, and

Jefferson's mother was also ill. He chose to stay with them, intending to return to Philadelphia only when his family was stronger. Jefferson kept up with the news from letters and newspapers. He read *Common Sense* by Thomas Paine. In the pamphlet, Paine wrote that "Tyranny, like hell, is not easily conquered; yet we have this consolation with us that, the harder the conflict, the more glorious the triumph." Like other Patriots, Jefferson was strongly moved by these words.

Jefferson's mother died of a stroke in March 1776. Jefferson stayed in Monticello another six weeks, afflicted with the severe headache that often accompanied his stress. He had hoped that Martha could return to Philadelphia with him. But in May, when he had to return to the Continental Congress, she was still not well. He made the one-week trip from Monticello to Philadelphia with his fourteen-year-old slave Bob Hemings.

During the six months he had been absent, events had pushed the colonies toward independence. In March, the Congress had sent a representative to France to negotiate for assistance against the British. In April, the Congress declared economic independence by opening American ports to trade of all nations except Britain. In March, South Carolina adopted a constitution that virtually declared its independence. In April, North Carolina instructed its representatives to the Congress to support independence. In May, Rhode Island did the same. The Provisional Congress of Massachusetts declared that towns in Massachusetts were ready to declare independence. Virginia followed suit. That same month, the Congress authorized the colonies to ignore the authority of the crown and to set up independent governments.

On June 7, 1776, Richard Henry Lee of Virginia introduced a resolution to the Congress calling for independence. This resolution did not receive easy acceptance. The delegates were still divided in their views on the colonies' relationship with England. Representatives from New York, New Jersey, and Pennsylvania, all under pro-British governors, were not ready to declare independence. Delegates from the New England colonies of Massachusetts, Maine, New Hampshire, and Connecticut supported independence. Delegates from Virginia and Georgia applauded the resolution. The debates were noisy and vehement. For the most part, Jefferson sat quietly, listening but not offering his opinion; his frequent demeanor in a controversial situation. Finally, representatives agreed to postpone the decision until July 1, hoping that some action or line of thought would provide an acceptable answer for all.

Some of Jefferson's thoughts were on his wife at Monticello, and others were on the Virginia legislature, which was creating the colony's new government. The legislature had already assigned a committee to write a draft of a new state constitution. Jefferson could not accept that such a document would be written without his input. Despite the responsibilities required by the

Congress, Jefferson took it upon himself to draft a constitution for Virginia.

The draft he sent to Williamsburg included a plan for separation of legislative, executive, and judicial powers. He advocated granting voting privileges to virtually every white male in Virginia, reducing the ownership of property requirement then in effect. In the two-house legislature that he proposed, the senate would be a body of men appointed by their peers in the house of representatives. He included abolition of importation of slaves, prohibition of an established church, and equal rights for males and females to inherit property and money. These were considered very radical proposals in the eighteenth century. In the constitution, Jefferson did not claim to reflect the opinions of all Virginians—or even the majority of them. About half of those who lived in Virginia were slaves with no right to vote; about one quarter were free white men who did not meet the voting requirement of owning land (a group that the new constitution would enfranchise); and of course, women could not vote.

In one section of the document, Jefferson outlined his thoughts on the difference between natural rights and civil rights. He defined natural rights as those that can be exercised by an individual, such as the right to think, speak, and give opinions freely. He defined civil rights as those which one exercises only with the consent of others, such as the right to own property.

Jefferson was highly disappointed to learn later that

for new-modelling the form of Government and for establishing the Fundamental principles thereof in future.

Whereas George   Guelf king of Great Britain and Ireland and Elector of Hanover heretofore entrusted with the exercise of the kingly office in this government hath endeavored to pervert the same into a detestable and insupportable tyranny;

by putting his negative on laws the most wholesome & necessary for ye public good

by denying to his governors permission to pass laws of immediate & pressing importance, unless suspended in their operation for his assent, and, when so suspended, neglecting to attend to them for many years;

by refusing to pass certain other laws, unless the persons to be benefited by them would relinquish the inestimable right of representation in the legislature

by dissolving legislative assemblies repeatedly and continually for opposing with manly firmness his invasions on the rights of the people;

when dissolved, by refusing to call others for a long space of time, thereby leaving the political system without any legislative head;

by endeavoring to prevent the population of our country, & for that purpose obstructing the laws for the naturalization of foreigners & raising the condition of new appropriations of lands;

~~in times of peace, standing armies & ships of war;~~

by ~~affecting~~ to render the military independent of & superior to the civil power;

by combining with others to subject us to a foreign jurisdiction giving his assent to their pretended acts of legislation

for quartering large bodies of troops among us;

for cutting off our trade with all parts of the world;

for imposing taxes on us without our consent;

for depriving us of the benefits of trial by jury;

for transporting us beyond seas to be tried for pretended offences; and

for suspending our own legislatures & declaring themselves invested with power to legislate for us in all cases whatsoever;

by plundering our seas, ravaging our coasts, burning our towns and destroying the lives of our people;

by inciting insurrections of our fellow subjects with the allurements of forfeiture & confiscation

by prompting our negroes to rise in arms among us; those very negroes whom ~~by an inhuman use of his negative he hath~~ refused us permission to exclude by law

by endeavoring to bring on the inhabitants of our frontiers the merciless Indian savages, whose known rule of warfare is an undistinguished destruction of all ages, sexes, & conditions of existence;

A draft of Jefferson's proposed constitution for Virginia, 1776.

only his preamble, a list of grievances against King George III, was accepted by the delegates. The preamble included a bill of rights, which stated, "all men are by nature equally free," "the enjoyment of life and liberty," and "government is, or ought to be, instituted for the common benefit."

Meanwhile, the representatives of the Second Continental Congress pondered, discussed, and debated the future of the colonies. These representatives were not rabble rousers. Almost all were men of property with a great deal to lose, and most were students of history, government, and philosophy. Jefferson, often called the foremost leader of the Age of Reason in America, wrote:

> It is honorable for us to have produced legislators who had the courage to declare that the Reason of man may be trusted with the formation of his own opinions . . . We believed that man was a rational animal . . . We believed that men, habituated to thinking for themselves, and to follow their reason as a guide, would be more easily and safely governed than with minds nourished in error and vitiated and debased by ignorance.

On June 11, Jefferson had scarcely finished working on his version of the Virginia constitution when he received an assignment from the Continental Congress: He was appointed to a committee charged with drafting a declaration of independence. In later years Jefferson and John Adams gave different stories of this assignment. Jefferson said that he alone was asked to write the Declaration of Independence. John Adams said that a committee was appointed to do the writing and that the committee chose Jefferson to actually draft the document.

However the assignment was made, it was thirty-three-year-old Jefferson, the youngest delegate from Virginia, who actually wrote the first draft of the Declaration of Independence in Philadelphia in June 1776. Every morning he awoke early and wrote in the coolness of the dawn. Then he took his seat in the Continental Congress at the State House, attended committee meetings, and listened attentively but spoke little.

In the afternoon he returned to his lodgings and wrote into the sultry evenings. Because he needed to dip his goose quill pen into an inkwell every word or two, his thoughts must have galloped way ahead of his hand. Perhaps no other representative would have taken this task so seriously. Jefferson had a great reverence for the power of the pen as well as a deep desire to see the colonies become independent.

Some words and phrases came more easily than others. He drew on his years of study of government and philosophy, particularly his admiration for the writing of John Locke, who had questioned the divine rights of kings and supported the rights of citizens to rebel. Because he had recently worked on a constitution for Virginia, much of the wording was on the tip of his pen. Jefferson wanted to tell the colonists, the British people and government, and, indeed, the whole world, that the colonists were a free people with long-established rights now being denied them by the king.

> When in the course of human events, it becomes necessary for a people to advance from that subordination in which they have hitherto remained, and to assume among the powers of the earth the equal & independent station . . . We hold these truths to be sacred and undeniable; that all men are created equal and independent . . . endowed by their creator with certain inalienable rights . . . We . . . reject and renounce all allegiance and subjection to the kings of Great Britain.

After about two weeks of writing, Jefferson showed his draft to Adams and Benjamin Franklin. Jefferson later wrote that these men made only two or three small corrections. Studies of this first draft show, however, that over twenty corrections were made, and three new paragraphs were added to create a second version.

Jefferson proudly presented a clean copy of the draft to the Second Continental Congress on June 28, 1776. It was read aloud and then placed on a table so the representatives could study it. Before they debated the declaration, however, the Congressmen first had to vote on the basic question of independence. For some representatives, this debate was exhilarating, an opportunity to voice their challenge to other representatives, to stand up and be counted as free-thinkers. For others, it

The committee to draft the Declaration of Independence included, from left to right: Benjamin Franklin, John Adams, and Thomas Jefferson. *(Courtesy of the Library of Congress)*

was frightening, an invitation to the British to find them guilty of treason and subject to a sentence of torture and then death. For some, it was a cruel choice between their ancestral allegiance to England and their future hopes for a brand new country.

After four tension-filled days, the debate ended on July 2 with a vote for independence. With emotions high, the Congress was ready to discuss the written declaration. Members of the Congress were all working together for the same goal, but each of them had a different constituency and different background. Could they achieve a consensus that would satisfy the needs of all the representatives? Jefferson later described the two and a half days of revision as a painful humiliation. Delegates debated every line, deleting and changing some of the major clauses in the original document.

Some delegates objected to Jefferson's attack against what he called the tyranny of the king. Jefferson had written: "He [the king] had suffered the administration totally to cease . . ." and Representatives substituted: "He [the king] has obstructed the administration of justice . . ."

Some criticized his paragraph in which he declared that the slave trade was "a cruel war against nature itself." How could an owner of slaves write this? Was slavery not necessary for the business of the nation? What was wrong with slavery, a source of labor that had contributed greatly to the prosperity of the colonies? Jefferson could not answer these questions to the satis-

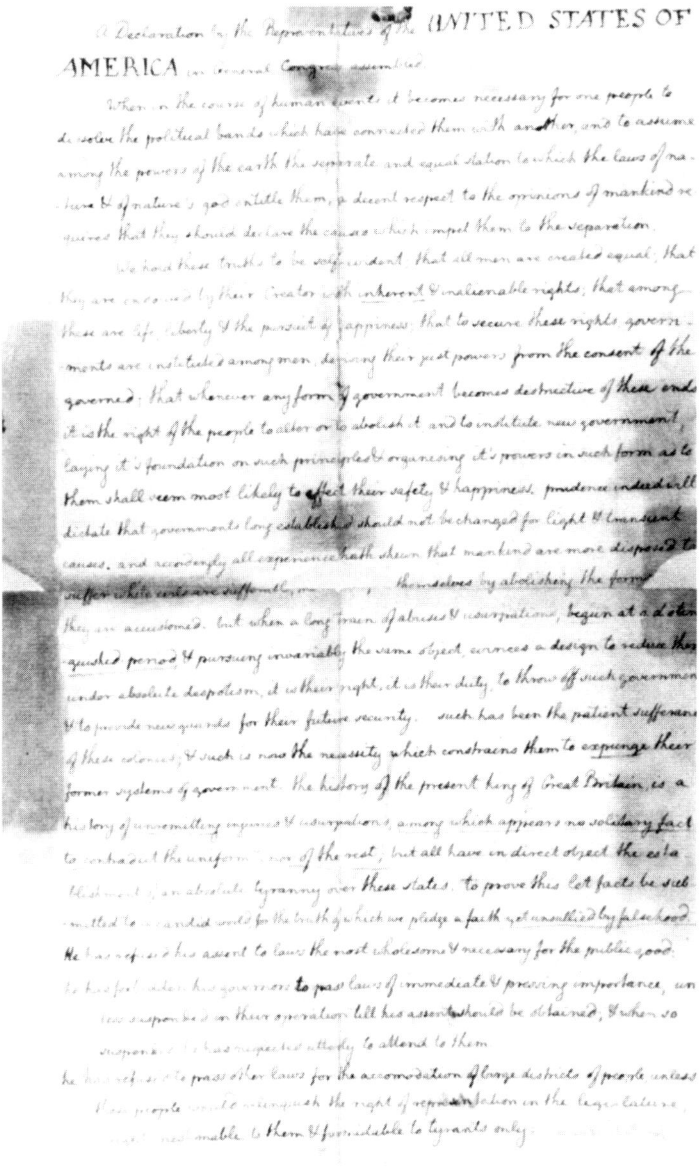

A Declaration by the Representatives of the UNITED STATES OF AMERICA, in General Congress assembled.

When in the course of human events it becomes necessary for one people to dissolve the political bands which have connected them with another, and to assume among the powers of the earth the separate and equal station to which the laws of nature & of nature's god entitle them, a decent respect to the opinions of mankind requires that they should declare the causes which impel them to the separation.

We hold these truths to be self-evident; that all men are created equal; that they are endowed by their Creator with inherent & inalienable rights; that among these are life, liberty & the pursuit of happiness; that to secure these rights governments are instituted among men, deriving their just powers from the consent of the governed; that whenever any form of government becomes destructive of these ends, it is the right of the people to alter or to abolish it, and to institute new government, laying it's foundation on such principles & organising it's powers in such form as to them shall seem most likely to effect their safety & happiness. prudence indeed will dictate that governments long established should not be changed for light & transient causes: and accordingly all experience hath shewn that mankind are more disposed to suffer while evils are sufferable, [illegible] themselves by abolishing the forms to which they are accustomed. but when a long train of abuses & usurpations, begun at a distinguished period & pursuing invariably the same object, evinces a design to reduce them under absolute despotism, it is their right, it is their duty, to throw off such government & to provide new guards for their future security. such has been the patient sufferance of these colonies; & such is now the necessity which constrains them to expunge their former systems of government. the history of the present king of Great Britain, is a history of unremitting injuries & usurpations, among which appears no solitary fact to contradict the uniform tenor of the rest, but all have in direct object the establishment of an absolute tyranny over these states. to prove this let facts be submitted to a candid world for the truth of which we pledge a faith yet unsullied by falsehood.

He has refused his assent to laws the most wholesome & necessary for the public good.

he has forbidden his governors to pass laws of immediate & pressing importance, unless suspended in their operation till his assent should be obtained; & when so suspended, he has neglected utterly to attend to them.

he has refused to pass other laws for the accommodation of large districts of people, unless those people would relinquish the right of representation in the legislature, a right inestimable to them & formidable to tyrants only.

The Declaration of Independence, 1776.

faction of delegates from South Carolina and Georgia, who felt they needed slaves to run their plantations. In the end, Jefferson acted ambivalent about slavery. The wishes of South Carolina and Georgia were heeded.

More questions shot out from the convention floor: Why was there no passage guaranteeing freedom of speech and freedom of the press? Why was there no statement affirming the right to protest against unfair courts? Jefferson insisted that defining these principles in writing would limit them in action. Delegates voted to delete Jefferson's passage that included "We must endeavor to forget our former love for them [the British], and to hold them . . . enemies in war, in peace friends."

Jefferson sat silently as criticisms flew and revisions were suggested, speaking only when others directly questioned him. In all, the representatives changed one-fourth of Jefferson's draft. In his journal, Jefferson criticized some of the deletions and additions, adding: "The pusillanimous idea that we had friends in England worth keeping terms with still haunted the minds of many." Although the revision process was painful, Jefferson knew that the delegates were generally in agreement with his declaration. But they needed to pick away at the manuscript until they felt sure that it was a document they could justify to their constituents and, more drastically, that they would risk their lives for.

On July 4, 1776, in a hot and crowded room of the Philadelphia State House, Congress voted on whether to accept the Declaration of Independence. The count was twelve affirmative votes and one abstention from New York. Congress ordered that the document be authenticated and printed. Only the president and secretary of the Congress, John Hancock and Charles Thomson, signed it.

The next day the printer had broadside editions of the declaration ready, and delegates sent copies to friends. On July 6, the *Pennsylvania Evening Post* printed the full declaration on the front page.

At noon on July 8, the sheriff of Philadelphia read

Members of the Second Continental Congress voted in favor of Thomas Jefferson's Declaration of Independence. *(Courtesy of the Library of Congress)*

the Declaration of Independence to crowds gathered in the State House yard. The rest of the day was filled with cheering and parades. In the evening, bonfires blazed and church bells tolled. New York City crowds smashed King George III's statue into a thousand pieces. In Baltimore, revolutionaries burned King George in effigy. In other colonies, replicas of the coat of arms of the crown were burned and torn into shreds. For several days, as the news of the declaration spread from colony to colony, demonstrations continued. On August 2, delegates signed the newly hand-lettered parchment that declared the birth of the United States of America.

Now Jefferson felt free to turn his thoughts to Monticello. He made two requests to the Congress. He asked that he be allowed to go home immediately to his ailing wife, and that he be allowed to resign his seat in the Congress as soon as possible. The group rejected both requests, but Jefferson, distraught with worry about Martha, resigned his seat without permission in September and left Philadelphia.

Chapter Five

Governor

Back in Monticello, Jefferson was relieved to find that his wife, although pregnant again, was not seriously ill. He promised her that he would stay in Virginia. He would not return to Philadelphia, but he would like to attend the Virginia assembly, which replaced the House of Burgesses, in Williamsburg. He could make the trip in less than a day on horseback. His fellow representatives had asked him to serve on a committee to revise the laws of the state of Virginia.

That summer, the British struck at New York City, and General Washington's troops lost control of the area. Then the British chased the Americans out of Long Island, across the Hudson River, and into New Jersey and Pennsylvania.

In October, Jefferson received an urgent message from John Hancock in Philadelphia saying that he had been chosen as commissioner to the court of France. Jefferson would be perfect, thought Hancock, because of his diplomatic skill, knowledge of French, and gift with words. But Jefferson turned down the offer because of Martha's pregnancy. He refused to be away from her, and she was physically unable to withstand the two-month voyage. Jefferson did not explain this situation to Hancock; he simply refused the appointment with a vague excuse. His refusal angered some representatives who, not knowing the details of Martha's delicate health, thought that Jefferson should sacrifice his own comfort for the post.

Jefferson remained steadfast in his resolution to stay close to Martha despite the intensification of the war. At Monticello, he worked for the cause in the only way he could: He helped collect blankets and winter clothing for the Patriot soldiers who were freezing in New Jersey in the coldest winter in memory. It was in New Jersey that Washington scored an impressive victory after crossing the icy Delaware River to make a surprise attack on the British at Trenton. Then, in the winter of 1777, the British failed miserably in their plan to conquer New York and isolate New England when they had to surrender their army in upstate New York.

Jefferson spent most of 1777 at home in Monticello, returning to Williamsburg just twice a year to work with the Virginia assembly. He fully enjoyed his family, his gardens, and his studies. He was at Martha's side in May when their son was born and seventeen days later when the boy died. Martha had now been pregnant three times, and only Patsy had survived. Jefferson tried to work out his grief by caring for his wife and

General George Washington led American soldiers across the icy Delaware River to secure a decisive victory over the British at Trenton. *(Courtesy of the Library of Congress)*

daughter and by completing further work on Monticello. He supervised the building of a portico, the making of 100,000 more red bricks, and, always, the creation and care of the garden and orchards. He always had new plans for grafting cherries, apples, pears, and other fruit. He continued to import trees and plants and was particularly pleased with an olive tree from Italy. When Jefferson discovered a burial mound on his land, he carefully removed and classified bones and teeth to create a record of the ancient society.

As Jefferson found new tasks to keep him busy at Monticello, the war continued with a new British offensive. Having failed to crush the revolution by conquering New York, the British now concentrated on crushing the southern colonies. They had faith in their superior numbers of troops and believed that they could build an offensive force quickly in the south. They were convinced that most people in the south remained loyal to the crown, and that they would assist the British once it was clear they would be protected from the Patriots.

British military leaders were wrong on both counts. The American military force in the south was quickly augmented by French ships, which prevented the British navy from freely patrolling the coast. Far from being Loyalists, most southern colonists supported the American cause and provided the American army with both food and intelligence about British maneuvers.

As the war moved closer, Jefferson remained with his family in Monticello. In August 1778, Polly was born. In November, when Jefferson felt assured that both mother and daughter were healthy, he returned to the Virginia assembly for some of the meetings. The usually conscientious and hard-working Jefferson did not attend every meeting and more than once he had to pay fines for his absences. A few friends scolded him for being inattentive at this crucial time. They did not know that Jefferson was torn between politics and his concern over Martha's health, and his growing interest and pride in Monticello. He solved these conflicts in part by doing some legislative work at home. He used his extensive library at Monticello to prepare papers.

One of his tasks was to reform Virginia's legal code.

In all, Jefferson wrote 126 bills, more than any other legislator. Many resolutions broke with tradition, such as his advocacy for the separation of church and state. In England and during the colonial period, the Anglican Church had always been supported by state taxes. He proposed free public schools for all, at a time when education had long been a privilege of the wealthy. He supported abolition of the death penalty, except in cases of murder or treason. He asked for modernization of the curriculum of the College of William and Mary. The assembly watered down most of his proposals, leaving Jefferson feeling discouraged.

During the winter of 1778-79, the Jefferson family became personally involved in the war when the Continental Congress ordered that citizens of Albemarle County supervise 4,000 British prisoners-of-war. Virginians were told to feed and shelter them as well as they could until the war ended and they could be freed. Most Virginians were outraged to be required to feed the enemy from their less-than-full storerooms. Jefferson viewed the situation in a different light. He looked forward to having conversations with the officers and to learning more about their backgrounds and future plans. He even became friendly with some of the officers, particularly the German officers who had been hired by the British crown. Jefferson invited these officers to spend evenings at Monticello. Although Jefferson could not speak German, he was able to converse with the prisoners in a combination of English, French, and Italian.

As the war continued in the southern colonies, it became clear that the Patriots had one distinct advantage over the British: They were defending their homeland. On the other hand, the British had a greater number of highly trained troops and superior weapons and equipment. British leaders made numerous mistakes. Perhaps most importantly, the British used European battle tactics which included lining up troops in open battlegrounds. Using guerilla tactics, the Americans were frequently able to harass these troops and force them to retreat. France's entry into the war on behalf of the Patriots in 1778 added to the Patriot advantage.

It is not surprising that in 1779 Jefferson was nominated for governor of Virginia. If elected, he would take the place of Patrick Henry, who was not allowed to run again. Thirty-six-year-old Jefferson was known and respected throughout America as the author of the Declaration of Independence. At home, he was respected for his work in the Virginia assembly and the Virginia Conventions. He had completed a detailed and workable revision of the laws of Virginia, helped to draft the new constitution of the state, and drafted the Bill for Religious Freedom.

When asked about the potential nomination, Jefferson seemed to dislike being pulled away from the "private retirement to which I am drawn by nature with a propensity almost irresistible." He spoke of his wife's frail health, his daughters, and his never-ending projects at Monticello. Many friends and other supporters begged him to accept. It would be difficult for any politician to refuse to run for governor of Virginia, the largest colony in America. The territory stretched westward all the way to the Mississippi River and included a population of about 500,000 whites and the same number of slaves. Politically, it was one of the most innovative and forward-thinking colonies. If a politician wanted to make a difference in the growth of America, and Jefferson did want to do that, Virginia was an excellent stage from which to act. He allowed his name to be put on the ballot, and he was elected by a vote in the Virginia assembly. Although he accepted the challenge, Jefferson admitted that he was not fully prepared to be chief administrator of a colony at war.

Before Jefferson was inaugurated, a small British naval force seized the harbor city of Portsmouth, Virginia, and spent sixteen days plundering the Virginia coast. Governor Jefferson had 50,000 militia men, but only 4,000 muskets. He was virtually helpless in the face of the British attack. After inflicting damage for more than two weeks, the British moved south in search of greater conquests.

Jefferson faced other serious problems as governor. Inflation was rising and legislators kept printing more and more money. They proposed new taxes—a poll tax, taxes on slaves, imports, and other goods, and taxes to pay for military clothing and munitions for the federal militia. These taxes were doomed before they were signed into law. Because of their experience with the crown, Virginia citizens were suspicious of centralized government. They were at war with England over taxation, and they were not going to accept new taxation from their local government.

Jefferson had a problem meeting the demands of the Continental Congress for men and military supplies to be sent to the national army. He had his own state militia to feed and arm, and Virginia barely had enough supplies for that. He placed an embargo on food grown in Virginia, planning to furnish his soldiers with Virginia-raised beef, pork, corn, wheat, and other basic foods as well as give them uniforms and munitions. But Jefferson could not stop the profiteers who managed to smuggle supplies out of Virginia and into the hands of those who would pay well for them. Problems also arose along the Virginia frontier as Native Americans and pioneers clashed over land and resources. And always there was the threat of another British invasion.

Jefferson's experience had accustomed him to working alone. He did not make as much use of his aides and department heads as he could have, instead falling back on a procedure that had worked for him when he was a member of the legislature: Jefferson wrote letters, hundreds of them. But the job of governor required face-to-face mediation, arbitration, arm-twisting, and give-and-take. Before he learned this lesson, Jefferson failed in two attempts to raise much-needed money for Virginia.

A highlight in his tenure as governor was appointing George Rogers Clark, a military leader and frontiersmen, to explore the sites where the Mississippi and Ohio Rivers came together. He asked Clark to map the territory and to foster a friendship with the Indians living there. Jefferson knew that, even in the midst of the approaching British military threat, this frontier would be important to Virginia. Clark followed Jefferson's instructions to ship to him any extra large mammal skeletons so he could study them.

At Jefferson's request, the capital of Virginia was moved inland to Richmond in April 1780. He thought the capital should be closer to the geographical center of the state. He also hoped to gain some political advantage from the move, because the new capital would be more accessible to western farmers who would appreciate Jefferson's background. The move gave him an opportunity to draw up plans for a new capitol building. He asked a French architect to create a model of a building exterior in classical style, while Jefferson himself drew the plans for the interior of the building. Jefferson wanted to create a mall of six public squares, each with a magnificent brick government building as a focal point. He recalled Roman buildings and the power and authority that architecture suggested, but war and other conflicts intervened before Jefferson could work on his dream.

In late October and early November 1780, British ships entered the harbor at Chesapeake. By the first week in November, about 3,000 British troops were concentrated in Portsmouth, a vital shipping town. Jefferson convened the council of state and asked that a standing army be created as soon as possible. The council thought this was an impetuous decision and refused to sanction it. In early January, Jefferson was awakened at dawn by a pounding at the door. A messenger told him that a British fleet had entered the James River and was headed toward Richmond.

Immediately, Jefferson told his servants to pack up emergency supplies—coats and shoes and a few necessities for the children, who now included infant Lucy Elizabeth. He settled his wife and daughters into a carriage and sent them off to nearby Tuckahoe. Saying he had no time, he ignored Martha's pleas to make arrangements for the slaves so they would not be left to the mercy of the invaders. Two days later in Richmond, Jefferson learned that a force of over 1,000 British soldiers was proceeding rapidly toward the capital. As fast as he could, Jefferson convened his council and ordered all possible militia to meet in nearby Westham. His call for militia brought only 200 men who had come to protect the governor, not to defend the city. Jefferson supervised the removal of as many supplies and government papers as he could from Richmond and then left the city to join his family.

A week later, Jefferson learned that the British troops had left the capital. He returned to find that they had set fire to his home, a newly-built munitions plant, and large stores of gunpowder, before moving south to inflict more damage. The British troops had been led by the Patriot-turned-traitor, Benedict Arnold, a colonel who had fought valiantly for the Americans at Quebec. Jefferson was so angry about this treachery that he offered a large reward to anyone who returned Arnold for sentencing.

Traitor Benedict Arnold aided the British in the war for independence. *(Courtesy of the Library of Congress)*

Instead of the sympathy he expected from Virginian patriots, Jefferson encountered questions and criticism. Why had he not ordered the Virginia militia to defend the city? Why did he leave Richmond instead of staying to defend it? Had Jefferson done all he could to defend the colony?

Jefferson had ready answers for the questions. He could not defend the city because, as requested by Congress, he had sent Virginia troops and arms to other colonies and had little left for his own use. He had left the city because he had no means to defend it. Yes, he had done everything he could do under the circumstances to defend Virginia. But emotions were high, tempers were quick, and fear was strong.

His political opponents insisted that the governor was a coward and an incompetent leader. For the next three months, Jefferson was widely and soundly criticized. Legislators showed their scorn by not showing up for executive sessions. Much of the time, the governor could not produce a quorum in the council to carry out any business, not even the business of raising arms and soldiers to defend Virginia.

Meanwhile, the war was not going well for the Americans. The British were in control of Georgia and South Carolina, and it seemed to be only a matter of time before they captured North Carolina. Virginia could be the next battleground for troops advancing from the south. Jefferson wrote letters to the Continental Congress warning of this potential disaster and begging for troops and supplies, but he received no help.

Jefferson was fed up. He decided to retire from the governorship in June 1781, the end of his second term. Before he could effect this resignation and return to Monticello, Lucy Elizabeth, less than five months old, died. The loss of three children sent Martha into such a deep depression that she was unable to carry on the management of the household. The tragedy added to Jefferson's decision to leave office.

Near the end of May, Richmond was again overrun by British soldiers. The Jeffersons retreated to Monticello accompanied by as many government officials as would come. Everyday, Jefferson and the officials traveled to nearby Charlottesville to carry on their work, returning each evening to Monticello to eat and to rest.

On June 4, Jefferson was awakened at sunrise by an aide who told him that a raiding force of British soldiers planned to capture him. After sending his wife and daughters to Blenheim, a nearby town, Jefferson ordered servants to hide the silver and other valuables. Suddenly he spotted the British coming up the mountain. He escaped to Blenheim and his family. While at Monticello, British troops ruined fields, burned barns, and stole horses, crops, and slaves.

Safe from this destruction, the Jeffersons waited to see what would happen next. Soon, they received word that General Thomas Nelson, commander-in-chief of the Virginia militia, was elected to replace Jefferson as governor. In the fall the legislature would conduct a formal inquiry into Jefferson's conduct in his last year in office. Jefferson was severely shaken by the criticisms of the legislature. He wrote to a friend, "I have retired to my farm, my family and books, from which I think nothing will ever more separate me."

In June, the Virginia assembly returned to the capital. As promised, one of their first moves after reconvening was to request that an inquiry be made into Jefferson's behavior as wartime governor.

Martha was pregnant again. Determined to be a conscientious husband and father, Jefferson became immersed in Monticello. He tended to his land and gardens and even began to collect notes and observations

Notes on Virginia, 1782.

for a book about gardening. His progress was slower than he had hoped because he fell off his horse and broke his wrist.

Without intending to, he started writing a book about Virginia. François de Barbé-Marbois, the French consul in Philadelphia, had written Jefferson a list of twenty-three questions about Virginia. Jefferson already had a formidable collection of records on everything from the weather and crops to his studies and judicial decisions. He found his scientific mind eager to compose lengthy answers to M. Marbois' questions, covering all matters such as boundaries, population, and natural resources. He also digressed into what he called the "tyranny of the clergy," the need for public education, and criticisms of the social and political aspirations of Virginians. He also wrote about slavery: "Indeed, I tremble for my country when I reflect that God is just, that his justice cannot sleep forever," and describing the present conflict he wrote: "I hope my countrymen will be sensible of it, and will apply, at a proper season, the proper remedy." His responses eventually became *Notes on Virginia,* a book that circulated both in America and in Europe.

On October 17, 1781, the British army under the command of Lord Cornwallis surrendered at Yorktown, Virginia, after George Washington took advantage of a British tactical error to stage a combined land and sea

Although Thomas Jefferson owned slaves, he wrote against the practice of slaveholding in *Notes on Virginia. (Courtesy of the Library of Congress)*

attack. Although there were still British troops in America, the war had become unpopular in England and it was clear that it was over.

Congress asked Jefferson to go to Europe to help negotiate the peace treaty. It was a tempting offer because it showed that members of the Continental Congress thought highly of him, even if many members of the Virginia assembly did not. But he refused to go because he knew that Martha's health was too fragile to make a trip across the Atlantic, and he could not bring himself to leave her. Instead, he decided that he would make one last political act: He planned to attend a meeting of the assembly to vindicate his actions as governor.

In November 1781, the Virginia legislature took up the matter of Jefferson's failure to defend Virginia from the British. Jefferson defended himself, charge by charge, and was acquitted. He returned to his beloved Monticello, vowing to never again become involved in politics. Once again his family and his home consumed his attention.

Chapter Six

Federal Appointments

In May 1782, Martha gave birth to another daughter, whom they named Lucy Elizabeth, after their baby who had died in infancy. Lucy Elizabeth fared well, but Martha grew weaker and weaker. Jefferson read to his wife, held her hand for hours, and willed her to live. He refused an offer to be a candidate for election to the Virginia assembly, but when voters elected him anyway, he refused to serve—his wife needed him, and he needed her.

News came back from Richmond that Jefferson might be arrested for refusing to serve in the legislature because he had been duly elected. Despite his desire to keep his family problems private, Jefferson felt compelled to admit that his reason for refusing to serve was his wife's health. Thirty-four-year-old Martha died soon after he gave his statement. Just before she died, she asked her husband not to marry again. She did not want her children to be brought up by a stepmother, as she had been. He promised.

Jefferson's grief was deep. For several months he refused to see anyone except ten-year-old Patsy. She accompanied him on walks and rode horseback with him for hours, often in complete silence.

Then Congress offered Jefferson a commission to negotiate the peace treaty in Paris. Feeling more in control of his emotions, he accepted. However, ice in the Chesapeake River prevented the sailing, and Jefferson missed signing the treaty.

Still, Jefferson was ready to get back into political life. When he learned that he had been elected to the Continental Congress again, he welcomed the opportunity. He began thinking and writing about his ideas for the constitution of Virginia, which had been rejected by the Virginia assembly in 1776. He was eager to discuss again his plan for creating a separation of the state's powers into three divisions—legislative, executive, and judicial. To him, a model government would have two legislative houses, a governor chosen by both houses of the assembly, freedom of religion and the press, and the end of capital punishment except in cases of treason, murder, or military offenses. He also proposed that after December 1, 1800, all slaves should be free.

Jefferson worked on more than political matters while waiting for the congressional session to begin. He catalogued his library of over 2,600 books, sorting them into three subjects: Memory, Reason, and Imagination. He began a classification of his letters using a polygraph, a new machine of his design, to make copies.

Once he had begun classifying his letters and papers, he found new uses for his personal records. He kept a daily journal of his garden, noting germination, blossoming, and growth. He kept an inventory of his 204 slaves. He admitted to close friends that his near-obsession with detail distracted him from his loneliness.

During this time he became close friends with a younger politician named James Madison. Like Jefferson, Madison was intrigued with the idea of creating a new government. The men talked for hours about roles for state and federal government. Both men were seeking to find a balance between authority and individual freedom in the new government. Their talks were enlivened by the difference in their personalities. Jefferson tended to be innovative, eager to find new ideas, and he was politically popular. Madison applied practical consideration to every idea, and he had little public magnetism.

That fall, Jefferson and eleven-year-old Patsy left for Philadelphia, where he would take up his duties with the Continental Congress. When the federal legislature moved to Annapolis, Maryland, Jefferson went with them, leaving Patsy in Philadelphia with a schedule that included practicing music from 8 a.m. until 10 a.m., studying dancing or drawing until 1 p.m., reading French from 3 p.m. until 4 p.m., more music from 4 p.m. until 5 p.m., and then reading and writing in English. He told her to write frequent and grammatically correct letters to her sister and to send a copy of each letter to him. He wrote, "If you love me then, strive to be good under every situation . . . towards ensuring you warmest love of your affectionate father."

Still depressed by Martha's death, Jefferson suffered from frequent migraine headaches. He wrote to a friend, "Having to my habitual ill health . . . lately added an attack of my periodical headach [sic], I am obliged to avoid reading, writing and almost thinking." In his autobiography he confided the source for his headaches— working with other legislators. He called the new representatives a group which "talks much and does nothing," lawyers "whose trade it is to question everything, yield nothing and talk by the hour." Despite his poor health, he headed many committees, wrote thirty-one reports and documents, and laid the foundation for an orderly expansion to the west. He was a member of nearly every important committee, even writing speeches and papers for some of his fellow delegates.

He was both praised and criticized for his proposal, called the Ordinance of 1784, which read in part: "After the year 1800 of the Christian era, there shall be neither slavery nor involuntary servitude." The proposal needed seven votes to pass. Although southern delegates voted against it, the measure garnered six votes, and Jefferson expected one more from Pennsylvania. But the Pennsylvania representative suddenly fell ill and could not vote, and the proposal was defeated. Afterward, Jefferson wrote: "The voice of a single individual . . . would have prevented the abominable crime [of sla-

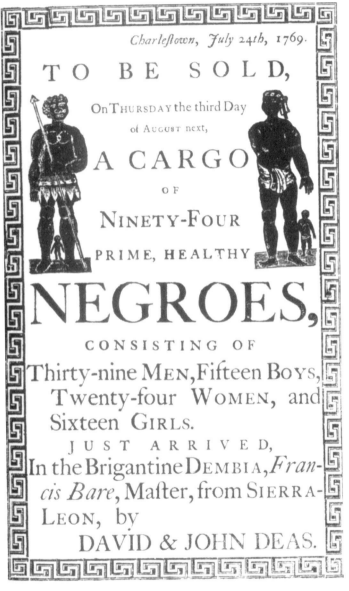

A 1769 broadside advertising the selling of slaves.
(Courtesy of the Library of Congress)

very] from spreading itself over the new country. Thus we see the fate of millions unborn hanging on the tongue of one man, and Heaven was silent in that awful moment."

That same year, Congress appointed him ambassador to work with John Adams and Benjamin Franklin in Europe. Their job was to negotiate treaties of commerce and friendship, and to organize the payment of America's debt to France for help during the Revolutionary War. Jefferson looked forward to learning more about international trade, and, perhaps more importantly, hoped he could better handle his grief over Martha's death if he were away from Virginia. Jefferson asked his sister-in-law to care for his two younger daughters, as he planned to take Patsy with him. On July 5, 1784, he and Patsy left Boston Harbor on the ship *Ceres*.

In Paris, Jefferson enrolled Patsy in a convent boarding school. With Patsy in school, he felt free to get to work and to appreciate his new surroundings. At first, he was thrilled with France—the beautiful bridges across the Seine River, meetings with Louis XVI and Frederick the Great, strolls in the Bois de Bologne and Tuileries, dinners and balls in high society. He loved the architecture, and he considered himself a lucky man to be in Europe at a time when people were intrigued by philosophy, history, art, music, and culture. He entertained on a grand scale, so grand that his income did not meet his expenses. He spent hours shopping, never hesitating to buy whatever took his fancy—

silver forks and spoons, wine, a new dress sword, clothing adorned with lace, as well as new clothes for Patsy and for his slave James Hemings. He spent half his salary buying fine furniture, renting a piano, hiring six additional servants, and buying a carriage that would have taken the average French laborer over seven months to pay for. Some weeks he bought books every day, adding 2,000 to his already large collection.

Jefferson's daughter Patsy accompanied him to Europe in 1784. *(Courtesy of the Library of Congress)*

At one point, he asked John Adams to help him get a personal loan from a Dutch bank. Adams helped, although he himself kept a close watch on his finances so that he never had to borrow.

The differences between the two men were perhaps even stronger than when they first met in Philadelphia in 1776. Jefferson was cool but amiable, a born diplomat who frequently managed to avoid confrontation without yielding to a basic demand. Adams was easily irritated, blunt, and uncompromising. Both were brilliant students of history and literature and firmly dedicated to their country.

After a few months, the thrill of being in France wore off for Jefferson. His negotiations about the importation of products from the United States—tobacco, rice, whale oil, and salted fish and meats—were often dry and frustrating. He was still full of despair over Martha's death. Then in January 1785, he was told that two-year-old Lucy Jefferson had died of whooping cough. Jefferson had now lost his wife and four of his children. It was without enthusiasm that he received the news that Congress had appointed him to succeed Benjamin Franklin as minister to the French court.

Jefferson succeeded Benjamin Franklin as minister to the French court in 1785. After Franklin returned to America, he presided over the Constitutional Convention, which was formed to replace the Articles of Confederation as the highest law of the United States. *(Courtesy of the Library of Congress)*

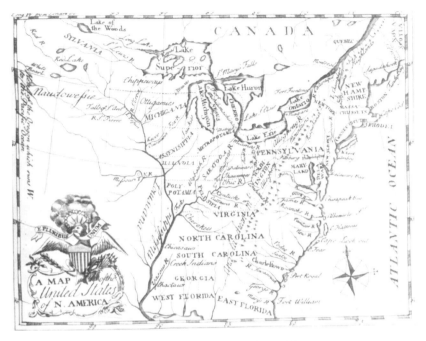

The United States of America, 1785.
(Courtesy of the Library of Congress)

Grieving, Jefferson resumed his diplomatic mission. Adams was a help to him, both in his sympathy for his losses and as a fellow diplomat with whom he shared many goals for their country. Jefferson worked on increasing the number of European markets for American raw materials and food and raising the status of America in the balance of European power. At every opportunity, he focused on his belief in free trade. Privately he cursed the British press that portrayed America as a riot-torn country on the brink of collapse. Competition between Great Britain and her former colonies further damaged an already unstable relationship.

The more Jefferson saw of European royalty, the more he respected what America could become as a democracy. He wrote to Washington, "There is scarcely an evil known in these countries which may not be traced to their king as its source . . ." He scorned European morals and gave this advice: "No American should come to Europe under 30 years of age."

In March 1786, he traveled to England to help John Adams, then the minister to the court of St. James, to negotiate a treaty on trade with the British. Jefferson was notorious in London for having attacked the king's divine right to rule. The king had called Jefferson an outlaw and said that he was guilty of treason. It was rumored that the king turned his back when Jefferson entered his presence and that Adams had to conduct his royal business without the aid of his friend. Although the rumor is probably false, Jefferson said later that "it was impossible for anything to be more ungracious" than his presentation at court. He reported to Congress: "That nation [England] hates us, their ministers hate us, and their king [hates us] more than all other men." He also said, "I consider the British our natural enemies." He proposed to shift American business away from Britain into France and other European countries as much as possible.

Jefferson was back into the swing of politics when his personal life took on a new twist. He met Maria Cosway, the wife of a famous painter. It may have been Maria's deep blue eyes and golden curls that first attracted him, but soon the couple spent almost every day together. They visited gardens and museums, and rode the city streets in his new carriage. He was a student of art; she painted portraits on commission. He loved his violin; Maria played both harp and harpsichord. They enjoyed many happy hours together, and provided topics for the gossips, before

Jefferson fell in love with Maria Cosway while he was in Europe. *(Courtesy of the Library of Congress)*

Maria left for Belgium with her husband.

In an effort to fashion a strong family bond with his remaining children, he asked that nine-year-old Polly come to France. She wrote back that she missed her father just as he missed her, but her solution to their loneliness was that he come to America to see her. She could not understand why her father had to be over 3,000 miles away if he really wanted to see her. Jefferson wrote to the relatives with whom Polly was staying. He encouraged them to trick her onto a transatlantic ship by saying that she could play there with one of his slaves, fourteen-year-old Sally Hemings.

The scheme played itself out. Polly and Sally played on the ship until the younger girl became tired and fell asleep. When she awoke, the ship was under sail. Sally and the kind crew helped Polly to overcome her anguish when she realized what had happened. By the time she reached France, Polly was eager to see her father and sister. Jefferson enrolled her in the convent with Patsy. The girls visited their father every weekend.

Concentrating on work again, Jefferson delved into the problems inflicted by pirates on American shipping. These pirates patrolled the coast of North Africa, called the Barbary Coast, which borders the countries of Morocco, Algiers, Tunisia, and Tripoli. Shipping on the coast was essential to American business. The United States exported a sixth of its wheat and flour and a quarter of its dried fish and rice to Mediterranean ports. The pirates demanded substantial payments from any ship using "their" waterway. If an American captain refused to pay, the pirates seized his ship and enslaved his crew.

Following his instincts to mediate first and threaten only if necessary, Jefferson succeeded in negotiating a treaty with Morocco. For a one-time payment of $30,000, Moroccan ships would not require American ships to pay tribute each time they used the waterway. But he was not able to negotiate with Algiers for the same kind of protection.

Jefferson was not satisfied with the news from the Constitutional Convention about its efforts to reform the Articles of Confederation, America's first constitution, which had been ratified in 1781. He wrote to many friends, including James Madison and George Washington, with suggestions about how the document could be revised. He wanted it to include a declaration of freedom of religion and the press, the right of *habeas corpus* to prohibit the unreasonable detention of a citizen, a trial by jury for any citizen accused of a crime, and a limit to the term of presidency. He sent messages to his supporters in America, urging them to insure that no ruler could be elected for life. He warned, "I was much an enemy to monarchy before I came to Europe. I am ten thousand times more so since I have seen what they are." When he learned of the growth of rebellious groups in America, he wrote: "The spirit of resistance to government is so valuable on certain occasions that I wish it to be always kept alive. It will often be exercised when wrong but better so than not to be exercised at all." He declared further that, "The tree of liberty must be refreshed from time to time with the blood of patriots and tyrants."

The growing resistance to the monarchy in France was also on Jefferson's mind. Frequent riots, sometimes leaving people dead, and a serious bread shortage were just two signs of an ominous future. He wrote to a friend: "The gay and thoughtless Paris is now become a furnace of Politics. All the world is politically mad. Men, women, and children talk nothing else." Jefferson wrote of the poverty of farmers he saw: "I observe women and men carrying heavy burdens and laboring with the hoe. This is an unequivocal indication of extreme poverty." This statement is puzzling in view of the fact that Monticello slaves did just that kind of work everyday.

Jefferson anonymously helped the Marquis de Lafayette, who was active in resisting the French king, to write the Declaration of the Rights of Man for presentation at the newly-formed French Assembly. In this paper, he advocated freedom of the press, freedom to choose a religion, unregulated commerce, freedom from false arrest, and strict regulation of the military. He also declared that no law, and certainly no constitution, could be considered inflexible: "No society can make a perpetual constitution or even a perpetual law." Jefferson listened proudly as the French National Assembly passed the Declaration of Rights in October 1789. He confidently predicted that this declaration would transform France.

He was wrong. The revolution had just begun. In June of that year, crowds rioted in the streets, first tearing down royal warehouses and buildings, and then destroying shops. Sixty thousand demonstrators marched on the Bastille, a prison well known for cruelty to prisoners, freed all the inmates, and tore down the structure. A few days later, crowds captured and hanged a minister of the king.

Soon it was no longer safe to live in Paris, and the Jeffersons left for America in October 1789. Along with furniture, statuary, and other art, Jefferson also brought enough books to fill 250 running feet of shelves. At the landing in Norfolk, a large delegation from the state

The notorious Bastille prison was stormed by French revolutionaries on July 14, 1789. *(Courtesy of the Library of Congress)*

assembly was on hand to greet them. In Richmond, both houses of the legislature loudly welcomed him back. When he arrived at Monticello, his slaves lined the path up the hill shouting greetings and cheers. Patsy later wrote, "When the door of the carriage was opened, they [the crowd] received him in their arms and bore him to the house, crowding around and kissing his hands and feet . . ." These genuine welcomes cheered him, but he still hoped to return to France once his daughters were settled safely in America.

Jefferson returned to find a great deal had changed in America while he was in Europe. The meeting called to revise the Articles of Confederation in 1787 had turned into a full-fledged Constitutional Convention. Lead by Jefferson's friend James Madison, New Yorker Alexander Hamilton, and others, the convention had worked throughout the hot summer to create a new government for a new country, the United States of America. Now there was a federal Congress divided into two houses, a federal judiciary, and a new executive branch headed by a president.

The first president of the United States was George Washington. The new president and fellow Virginian wanted Jefferson to remain in the United States and serve as the first secretary of state. This meant Jefferson would be in charge of organizing and implementing foreign policy.

Jefferson had a difficult decision to make. He could return to the sophisticated and lively life of Europe or

Secretary of State Jefferson differed with Secretary of the Treasury Alexander Hamilton on almost every issue facing the new nation. *(Courtesy of the Library of Congress)*

remain in the still primitive towns of Virginia and most of America. He told Washington that he much preferred to return to France, but he would remain in America if Washington insisted.

Jefferson assumed the office of secretary of state in March 1790. Almost from the beginning he found himself in bitter conflict with Secretary of Treasury Alexander Hamilton. Hamilton, fourteen years younger than Jefferson, was an intensely ambitious politician with support from the merchants and bankers in New York and other large cities. Their political differences were many. Jefferson favored close ties to France; Hamilton wanted close ties with England. Jefferson insisted that the best government was the smallest government; Hamilton favored a larger central government. Jefferson wanted each state to pay its own war debts; Hamilton wanted the national government to assume these debts. Jefferson supported cooperation of American and European navies against pirates; Hamilton supported paying tribute. Jefferson cheered French revolutionaries; Hamilton believed that the French revolution was ill-conceived and improper. Over the next few years the conflict between these two popular and charismatic leaders was instrumental in the development of the nation's first political parties. Those who favored Jefferson's views began to call themselves Republicans, and later Democratic-Republicans; Hamilton's supporters called themselves Federalists.

After only a month on his new job, Jefferson was

almost overcome with migraines that he said, "came on every day at sunrise and never left me till sunset." He was also annoyed by President Washington, who insisted on supervising him closely. He seriously considered retiring.

When Jefferson became convinced that Hamilton was embezzling treasury funds and sharing illegal proceeds with his family, he decided to stay and fight Hamilton publicly. He entered the fight full-throttle. Soon he was paying journalists to praise him and to write attacks on Hamilton. In retaliation, Hamilton, writing under a pseudonym, called Jefferson a poisonous snake, an instigator of national disturbances, and an ambitious revolutionary. Washington tried in vain to get the two men to stop quarreling.

In December 1792, Jefferson decided to make public the fact that Hamilton had engaged in a sexual affair and that he was paying bribes to the woman's husband to keep it secret. Jefferson was playing with fire. Many American and French officials knew of Jefferson's affair with the married Maria Cosway, and rumors were wide-spread that he had fathered at least one child by Sally Hemings, the young slave girl who had come to Paris as a maid to his daughter Polly. Apparently Jefferson decided that he would risk the public exposure of his own moral lapses if he could bring Hamilton down with him.

To work out his plan, Jefferson told Washington that he would stay on the job until autumn of 1793. Then he prepared accusations against Hamilton for lying to Congress, manipulating the financial markets, and working against the public interest. Hamilton composed brilliant replies to all the accusations and was acquitted by the House.

Chapter Seven

Vice President

In the midst of Jefferson's fight with Hamilton, relations with France deteriorated. The new French republic, which had temporarily emerged from the chaotic French Revolution, sent Ambassador Edmond Genet to America to present his credentials. Citizen Genet, as he preferred to call himself, angered many in the U.S. by arranging for the equipping of ships that would be manned by American sailors to work for the French government. He recruited Americans to fight against the Spanish, who claimed territory in Florida. Many saw this as an affront to American sovereignty. Jefferson wanted to develop good relations between the U.S. and the new government in France. Twice he warned Genet not to interfere with American neutrality. Twice Genet rejected the warning and even told Jefferson that he was planning to recruit an American army to invade Spanish-held Louisiana.

In 1793, the French captured a British ship, the *Little Sarah*, and towed it into Philadelphia. They planned to

Citizen Genet later became an American citizen. *(Courtesy of the Library of Congress)*

arm the ship and use it for French conquests. President Washington ordered the Supreme Court to define guidelines on neutrality: Should the United States government allow one country to attack another country's ship on its territory? The Court refused to consider the question. The cabinet voted unanimously to demand that Genet be recalled to France. The French government, which had changed since Genet had been sent to America, sent a replacement minister who brought orders for Genet's arrest. However, President Washington refused to extradite Genet because of the likelihood he would be executed in Paris. Genet eventually became an American citizen and settled in the United States.

Despite Washington's protests, Jefferson resigned as secretary of state at the end of 1793. Fifty-year-old Jefferson told a friend that he needed "to be liberated from the hated occupation of politics." He said that this would be a permanent retirement for him.

Some Federalists said that this was a very clever move aimed at furthering his political ambitions. They thought Jefferson had set his sights on the presidency. John Adams said, "Jefferson thinks by this step to get a reputation as an humble, modest meek man . . . He may even have deceived himself into this belief."

Whatever the truth, Jefferson looked forward to repairing, restoring, and renovating his estate. He also hoped to pay off the debts that had been steadily mounting. He intended to spend his time with his daughter Patsy, his son-in-law, and new granddaughter born to his daughter Polly. He wrote to a friend, "I have returned with infinite appetite, to the enjoyment of my farm, my family, and my books."

He wanted to devise a system of crop rotation, plant 900 peach trees, supervise his slaves, begin production of iron nails (with hopes of making enough money to pay some of his mounting debts), and double the size of the estate at Monticello. His kitchen garden included over 250 varieties of vegetables and herbs and twenty varieties of peas. At each corner of the house, he planted flower gardens in oval-shaped beds. He set aside nearly eighteen acres for trees, including groves of tulip poplars, copper beech, sugar maple, and dozens of other varieties. His six-acre fruit garden included figs, strawberries, and over 170 varieties of other fruits. He also modernized his farming implements and made a plow in a design which won him a gold medal from the department of agriculture in Paris.

To double the size of the house itself, Jefferson tore off the second floor. He wanted the building to be remodeled in the elegant style of Hotel de Salm, a residence he had admired on the left bank of the Seine in Paris. He admitted, "Architecture is my delight, and putting up and pulling down, one of my favorite amusements." In his twenty-one-room mansion he included many French innovations—beds in alcoves, elongated windows, a parquet floor—and he decorated with mirrors, clocks, and furniture he had shipped from France.

Several years later he wrote to his daughter that he had been mistaken in his belief that the challenges of Monticello would suffice to make him contented. "I am convinced our own happiness requires that we should continue to mix with the world, and to keep pace with it. I felt enough of the effect of withdrawing from the world then to see that it led to an antisocial and misanthropic state of mind, which severely punishes him who gives in to it."

Gradually, Jefferson moved back into political life, although he did not admit it publicly. He helped to create a national newspaper, *The National Gazette*, which published attacks on Hamilton and praised Jefferson.

Jefferson also maintained a running criticism of President Washington. When Great Britain declared war on France, Jefferson said that Washington should have sided with the French instead of declaring a proclamation of neutrality. When United States ambassador John Jay signed a treaty with England in 1794, Jefferson declared that Washington had made too many concessions to the British. When Hamilton, then secretary of the treasury, persuaded Washington to create a national bank, Jefferson insisted that a national bank would give the central government too much power.

In 1796, Washington refused a third term as president. The Republicans nominated Jefferson to run against Federalist Vice President John Adams. Jefferson accepted the nomination but refused to campaign. He said that he did not want the job, and that he was accepting the nomination only because he believed that the government needed a strong hand to swing it back to Republican ideals. Not everyone believed him: Most political leaders suspected that he was hoping to be elected president.

Political parties showed their strength in this election, unlike the first two in which Washington was elected unopposed. Adams and the Federalists called for a strong central government. They accused Jefferson of mismanaging the office of Virginia governor and of showing too much support for the French revolutionaries. On the other hand, Jefferson and the Republicans called for strong states' rights. When the old charges of his failure as Virginia governor were brought up, Republicans explained that Jefferson had been handicapped by a lack of troops and supplies. They supported his advocacy of the rights of common people to rebel when necessary, as had happened in the American and French revolutions.

Citizens did not vote directly for president and vice president. Writers of the Constitution believed that a group of electors, called the electoral college, should mark the ballots, trusting that the electors would not be swayed by partisan politics. Article II, Section I of the Constitution stated that each state legislature would choose its electors. Each elector would vote for the two candidates he deemed most qualified, and the two receiving the most votes would become president and vice president. Jefferson believed that he would be one of these top two. He said he would be happy with the vice presidency: "The second office is honorable and easy. The first is but splendid misery." Hamilton tried to persuade electors to vote for anyone other than Adams or Jefferson.

In December, Madison wrote to Jefferson at Monticello telling him that it looked as though Adams would win the presidency. Jefferson wrote to Adams, saying that he was glad to hear of his victory and wishing, "your administration may be filled with glory and happiness . . ." Just before Jefferson sent the letter he had second thoughts, and sent it to Madison for his opinion. Madison quickly explained to Jefferson that he must separate friendship and politics. Adams did not have to be reminded of Jefferson's friendship; their political relationship should remain flexible in case Adams' presidency did not warrant Jefferson's praise. In the end, Jefferson did not send the letter.

One hundred thirty-nine votes were cast by electors, and Adams won by three. On March 2, 1797, Jefferson was inaugurated as vice president. He was surrounded

Jefferson and James Madison agreed on many basic issues of government.
(Courtesy of the Library of Congress)

by banners reading, "Jefferson, the friend of the people."

This "friend of the people" had only one constitutional responsibility, and that was to preside over the Senate. With his usual enthusiasm for writing, classifying, and documenting, Jefferson expanded this responsibility. He wrote a parliamentary handbook (that is still used today) to help organize the procedures in the Senate. Adams did not invite him to take part in the workings of government. Although they had been good friends, their separate political views had driven a wedge into their relationship. Jefferson became restless. He wrote to Patsy in December 1797: "It gives me great regret to be passing my time so uselessly, when it could have been so importantly employed at home."

Because he was not busy with vice presidential responsibilities, Jefferson carved out a role for himself as unofficial head of the Republican party. One of his chief aides in this task was Aaron Burr of New York. Among other issues, Jefferson wanted his party to stand for states' rights. He wrote, "It is of immense consequence that the States retain as complete authority as possible over their own citizens." He believed that neither Adams nor Hamilton believed in the dignity of the common man as he did, and he feared that these leaders would try to strengthen the power of the central government at the expense of individual freedom.

War between England and France was the cause of an international incident in 1797. French privateers captured half a million dollars worth of American shipping on the pretext that they believed the Americans intended to sell the cargo to England to help them in the war against France. French envoys, dubbed X, Y, and Z, demanded a payment of $250,000 in return for smoothing relationships between France and America. This was an outright bribe, and American envoys exposed the fraud. The so-called "XYZ Affair" threatened to escalate to war between the U.S. and France. With the blessing of outraged American businessmen, the Federalist government suspended commerce with France, authorized seizure of French vessels, and called for a provisional army. Their rallying cry became "millions for defense but not one cent for tribute."

Jefferson acknowledged that French attacks on American shipping were contemptible, but he argued that Britain was also guilty of attempting to intimidate American shipping. He advocated neutrality toward both nations. He was too politically astute to attack Adams's policies directly, but he sent out hundreds of letters deploring America's military threats against France.

Many politicians, especially Republicans, saw this as the beginning of an attempt by Jefferson to oust Adams and gain the presidency for himself. Adams's supporters who had seen some of this literature warned the president to be on guard. Adams told his son about Jefferson: "I am obliged to look upon him as a man whose mind is warped by prejudice and so blinded by ignorance as to be unfit for the office he holds." Adams's and Jefferson's criticism of each other led to party divisions so strong that some described Jefferson's attacks as a call for another revolution.

Jefferson remained at Monticello with half of his mind on renovations to his estate and the other half on the national political situation. From Monticello he sent messages throughout the country. He sounded a call for peace and non-involvement in international disputes: "We owe gratitude to France, justice to England, good will to all, and subservience to none." With statements such as this, Jefferson achieved two goals: He criticized Adams, and he implied that he could handle the situation more effectively. Increasingly, politically aware citizens saw these messages as part of a campaign by Jefferson to become president.

Jefferson became more intense in his involvement when Congress passed the Alien and Sedition Acts in 1798. Until that time, aliens, or foreigners, such as Citizen Genet, could apply for citizenship after five year's residence in America. The Alien Act required fourteen year's residence before applying for citizenship. The acts gave the president the right to expel any foreigner whom he considered dangerous. Jefferson argued that because the United States was founded by immigrants, it should not impose harsh restrictions on citizenship. He argued that no single person, president or not, should have the power to expel another from the country.

The Sedition Act stated that any written or spoken attack against the government that could be judged to be "False, scandalous, and malicious" was punishable by fine and imprisonment. This was a severe limitation on the first amendment's guaranteed right to freedom of speech. Besides the fundamental wrong imposed by the acts he abhorred, Jefferson feared that Adams and other Federalists would use the acts as a way to silence, and possibly even exile, active Republicans. He soon had evidence to support this claim. In a few short months, the acts resulted in the prosecution of at least twenty-five writers, editors, and printers, most of whom were Republicans.

Jefferson saw the Alien and Sedition Acts as a prelude to stronger, all-controlling central government, and less freedom for both states and individuals. He began what he hoped would be a revolution of opinion. He secretly helped to draft the Kentucky and Virginia Resolutions of 1798, assisting those state legislatures to declare that the acts were unconstitutional and a gross distortion of federal authority. He urged that states react with nullification, the act of making a resolution null and void, by simply refusing to obey it. Adams answered publicly that it was the state resolutions, not the Alien and Sedition Acts, that should be nullified.

As Jefferson continued to stay in the public eye with denunciations of Adams, he paid journalist James Callendar to do all he could to defame the president. Few knew that Jefferson was funding the attacks. Publicly, Jefferson declared that he was disgusted with politics. He said he had family, financial, and emotional needs which could be met only at Monticello. But his actions did not match his words.

In early 1798, Jefferson continued to write hundreds of letters and political pamphlets criticizing Adams and suggesting that he had better answers for the questions that faced the nation. The letters went to potential supporters and the pamphlets were circulated widely in newspapers. In the summer of that year, Jefferson privately encouraged mass Republican demonstrations in Virginia and Kentucky, demanding that Congress repeal the laws. That summer and fall, he entertained hundreds of visitors, both committed and potential supporters, at Monticello.

In the spring of 1799, Madison and Jefferson made a concerted effort to strengthen the Republican party. They reminded voters that the Alien and Sedition Acts were due to expire in March 1801 and that it was essential that Republicans be in office at that time to make sure that the acts were not reinstated.

Jefferson and Madison were superb party organizers. They encouraged supporters in the Congress to get out the vote by pushing through election reform. They delegated campaigning chores to supporters in Congress and to other political officers. When Jefferson finally announced his intention to run, a strong party machine stood behind him.

New York Senator Aaron Burr, a Republican, was also nominated. The agreed upon plan was to elect Jefferson president and Burr vice president. The Federalists nominated John Adams and southerner Charles Coatsworth Pinckney. A two-party system was emerging, although most politicians claimed to be against factions.

One buzzword of Jefferson's campaign was "nullification." Republicans declared that this was a simple expression of the dominance of states over the federal government. Federalists declared that nullification was a Republican plan to overthrow the national government. Both sides brought up the name of King George III in their arguments. Republicans insisted that all the blood of the revolution could have been averted if colonists had been able to declare that King George's taxes were null and void. Federalists insisted that central authority had been necessary to defeat the British troops and to organize the colonies into a nation. Adams's party believed that a state-run church should establish statewide morals. Jefferson believed that individuals should use reason, not religious organizations, to determine morals.

Federalists declared that Jefferson was an immoral atheist. They talked about his love affair with Maria Cosway and hinted that he had sex with a slave on his estate. Republicans praised Jefferson's devotion to the common man and said that he demonstrated this in his support of the French Revolution. Adams, they argued, wanted to stifle freedom of the press, while Federalists shot back that Jefferson's laissez-faire attitude toward the press was excessive and dangerous.

By December, it was clear that the Republicans would win over the Federalists. But which Republican—Jefferson or Burr—would win the most votes and become president? Controversy swirled right up until the day the electors' votes were counted. As vice president, it was Jefferson's job to open the votes in front of Congress. He read out the tally—seventy-three votes for Jefferson, seventy-three votes for Burr, sixty-five for Adams, and sixty-four for Pinckney.

The Constitution dictated that the House of Representatives would decide the winner. Jefferson fully expected Burr to step aside and accept the vice presidency, but Burr refused to do so. Jefferson felt betrayed and now had a new enemy to go on his list along with Hamilton and Adams. Because Burr did not concede, the tension was drawn out over days. One representative, declaring that he was too ill to come in to vote, was carried in on a cot. Fully-dressed representatives slept in chairs on the floor of Congress. Hamilton was torn between voting for Jefferson, whom he called "a mischievous enemy . . . not scrupulous . . . a contemptible hypocrite . . ." or for Burr, whom he described "as unprincipled and dangerous a man as any country can boast . . ." Finally, he decided that Jefferson was the lesser of the two evils. On the sixth day and thirty-sixth ballot, Jefferson was elected president of the United States, and Burr was elected vice president.

Chapter Eight

President

The three previous presidential inaugurations had been filled with pomp and ceremony, but Jefferson said that he always walked to the capitol when he had business there, and he saw no reason to change that procedure on inauguration day. On March 4, 1801, accompanied by a group of friends, he strolled along muddy Pennsylvania Avenue in a plain dark suit. Only the artillery marching ahead of him indicated that this day was different from others. Punctual as usual, Jefferson climbed the steps of the capitol just in time for the ceremony at noon.

Rumors were widely spread that Adams refused to speak to Jefferson after the election. In fact, Adams invited Jefferson to dinner shortly after, Jefferson accepted, and the visit was amiable. However, Adams did leave Washington at four o'clock on the morning of the inauguration, either unable or unwilling to watch his opponent take office. Adams expressed relief that he was finally leaving Washington. He said, "If I were to go over my life again, I would be a shoemaker rather than an American statesman."

In his usual soft voice that few could hear, the new president promised that there would be no reprisals against those who had opposed him. He declared that he was a man of peace, a person who chose harmony over conflict. He said he wanted to blur the hard and fast lines of opposing political parties. "Every difference of opinion is not a difference of principle . . . We are all republicans—we are all federalists." He also restated his view that minorities had rights just as the majority did, that all men were created equal and entitled to life, liberty, and the pursuit of happiness. He pledged "peace, commerce and honest friendship with all nations, entangling alliances with none." He emphasized his commitment to promotion of states' rights and advocated thrift in government. He expressed support for agriculture, repeated his belief in freedom of religion, the press, and jury trial. He ordered a halt to all prosecutions under the Alien and Sedition Acts and a refund of all fines paid under that statute. Throughout his speech, Jefferson praised the spirit of liberalism, placing the individual citizen above all parties and forms of government.

James Madison became secretary of state, head of the patent office, issuer of passports and copyrights, and a liaison with territorial governments. As a cabinet officer, he had the responsibility of conveying American policy to ministers and consuls abroad. He con-

Jefferson did not delegate many responsibilities to Vice President Aaron Burr.
(Courtesy of the Library of Congress)

ferred daily with Jefferson on a number of subjects not limited to foreign policy. The pair declared that they envisioned the opening of a new era where the rights of all mankind would be respected and the potential of self-government would become reality.

One of Jefferson's first problems arose immediately. For weeks before the election, Adams had made many appointments, including 216 judicial officers—sixteen new circuit judges, many clerks and attorneys, and many justices of the peace. With Jefferson's full agreement, the Republican press criticized these appointments, calling them "midnight judges." They declared that Adams had made the appointments at the last minute in order to throttle the new administration. Federalists, including Adams, insisted that the appointments had been seriously studied for weeks, some for months, but Jefferson instructed Madison to withhold the official letters of appointment.

President Jefferson insisted that he had a right to hire and fire his own appointees. He asked Congress to repeal the Judiciary Act of 1801 that, Adams argued, permitted the appointments. With Jefferson's request, both the executive and legislative branches were involved in the question. He had no intention of involving the judicial branch, but it was brought into the conflict when William Marbury, who had been appointed as a magistrate by Adams, sued Madison for refusing to place him in his new job.

Now that all three branches of government were in-

In the landmark case, *Marbury v. Madison*, Chief Justice John Marshall ruled that in matters dividing government branches, the Supreme Court would make the final decision. *(Courtesy of the Library of Congress)*

volved, the Supreme Court under Chief Justice John Marshall—an Adams appointee and enemy of Jefferson— broadened the issue: If any branch of government disagreed with another branch, who would make the final decision? In a landmark case entitled *Marbury v. Madison*, the Court ruled that in a situation such as this, the Supreme Court would have the final decision. It then ruled that Adams's appointments would not stand. Although he was able to stop the "midnight judges" from assuming office, Jefferson was angered by the way the decision was made. The Court had given itself the right of "judicial review," or the power to declare any law passed by Congress to be unconstitutional. The Court also could assume the role as chief arbiter over state laws. Jefferson feared the Supreme Court had too much power.

As soon as Jefferson took office, he began what he later called the Revolution of 1800. He cut away at Federalist laws. The new president did not wait for Congress to initiate bills; he sent them many messages, telling them where to focus their energies. He worked to undercut the national bank and continually recommended slashes in federal spending. His theory was that no government had the right to incur debts that another generation would have to pay off. He cut the peacetime military force from 5,400 men to 3,300 men. He ordered construction of four ships fitted for patrolling the Mediterranean to stop pirating of American ships. He created the United States Military Academy at West Point. Jefferson may have believed that he was a pacifist, but as far back as 1776, when he worked on the Declaration of Independence, he believed that a defensive war was sometimes necessary for survival as a free people.

The Louisiana Territory was another problem facing Jefferson as he entered office. The French had originally claimed Louisiana, but they had given the territory to Spain as part of the treaty ending the French and Indian War. Then in 1800, French leader Napoleon Bonaparte secretly arranged that the territory be given back to France. During this time, American interest in the territory increased as settlers moved west. The Mississippi River was an important route for trade, and the port of New Orleans was especially important for temporary storage of imports and exports.

When he heard of the secret treaty that would return Louisiana to the French, Jefferson feared that France would use it as a foothold to build a colonial empire in the American West. This would probably force him to establish an unwanted alliance with Britain against France. Then a Spanish officer in New Orleans declared

that America could no longer use the port as a deposi-
tory for goods. Leading Federalists in Congress demanded that America go to war against Spain. Publicly,
Jefferson said that he refused to consider war. Secretly,
he ordered that infantry and artillery be stationed on
the Mississippi near the Spanish border. In return, Federalists demanded an immediate investigation of the
Louisiana affair. In a secret session, the House defeated
the resolution and affirmed Jefferson's actions in Louisiana. The situation was quiet for a short while but was
neither finished nor forgotten.

Just two months after he was inaugurated, Jefferson
faced another foreign policy crisis. The North African
country of Tripoli had attacked American ships in the
Mediterranean. Normal
government procedure
would assign this problem
to the state department.
Jefferson believed that the
solution was to order the
navy to destroy pirates
wherever they could be
found, even outside the
sea boundaries of Tripoli.
Sure of himself, Jefferson
ignored the state depart-
ment and took his ideas
straight to his cabinet, but
they would not sanction

Pirates off the coast of Tripoli attacked
American ships. *(Courtesy of the Library of
Congress)*

by-passing the state department. They insisted that the plan be reviewed by Congress, which was then on a seven-month vacation. With this matter, as with all others, Jefferson ignored the advice of Vice President Burr.

In Europe, Jefferson had grown to hate diplomatic protocol, which he sometimes called "diplomatic pretense." As president of the United States, he often received guests, including ambassadors and other official visitors, in old, sometimes shabby, clothes. His outfits shocked many distinguished guests, including British minister Andrew Merry, who arrived at the executive mansion in full diplomatic dress and was disturbed to find Jefferson wearing slippers. A Senator expressed surprise at finding Jefferson "drest, or rather *undrest*, with an old brown coat, red waistcoat, old corduroy small clothes, much soiled—woolen hose——and slippers without heels." Formal dinner parties were an exception. There Jefferson wore appropriate dress, and he lightly powdered his hair. He paid strict attention to the details of creating menus, preparing food, and serving wines.

Although Jefferson attempted to limit government spending, he was so lavish in his own personal spending that his debts mounted continually. His salary as president was $25,000, but he had to borrow $4,000 his first year in office to balance his personal budget. In another contradiction of Jefferson's personal behavior and his governmental attitudes, he relied more and more on slave labor for income at Monticello while he pub-

Negotiations for the purchase of the Louisiana Territory were undertaken by (from left to right): French finance minister François de Barbé-Marbois, James Monroe, and Robert Livingston. *(Courtesy of the Library of Congress)*

licly opposed slavery as a national disgrace, although he considered abolition of the slaves irresponsible. He said, "As far as I can judge from the experiments which have been made, to give liberty to, or rather, to abandon persons whose habits have been formed in slavery is like abandoning children."

The problem with the Louisiana Territory was still with him. Jefferson had received an offer from France to buy New Orleans and all Spanish territory east of the Mississippi for $6 million, plus a renouncement of all claims to land west of the Mississippi. Jefferson would never give up rights to all land west of the Mississippi, but he sent James Monroe, governor of Virginia, to France as a special envoy with authorization to buy New Orleans.

Napoleon's response to Monroe was far better than

Jefferson had expected. Before the Americans could mention money, Napoleon offered the territory of Louisiana from the Mississippi to the Rocky Mountains for about $15 million. (The Americans did not know then that Napoleon had given up on the idea of establishing colonies in America. He had turned his attention to settling the Caribbean.) He did not ask for prohibition of further American expansion into the West.

As he worked out a final draft of the treaty, Jefferson faced a conflict between his long argued belief in individual rights and self-government. Would he allow the French and Spanish citizens and the Native Americans in the territory to create their own government? The answer was no, he decided. He thought that he had always qualified his belief in self-government with a caveat about citizens needing a certain degree of education and understanding about democracy before they could hope to succeed. He did not feel that the people living in the area had that understanding.

Still another dilemma arose about the Louisiana Purchase, this one a constitutional dilemma. The Constitution did not outline the procedures for acquisition of new territory. Jefferson feared that a protracted argument in Congress could kill the deal: Napoleon might change his mind before the treaty could be ratified. So Jefferson decided to base his purchase on the constitutional authority given the president to make treaties with foreign nations. With this as a basis for his action, he sent the treaty to the Senate for ratification. The Federalists immediately set up a clamor about a president acting beyond his authority. However, they too thought the price was a bargain. Moreover, this situation created a potential political advantage: In the next presidential election, Federalists could accuse Jefferson of abusing the Constitution. After two days of debate, Senators ratified the treaty, thus doubling the size of American territory from 900,000 to 1,800,000 square miles.

In his annual message to Congress in December 1802, Jefferson proudly announced:

> Another year has come around, and finds us still blessed with peace and friendship abroad; law, order, and religion, at home, good affection and harmony with our Indian neighbors; our burdens lightened, yet our income sufficient for the public wants, and the produce of the year great beyond example.

Early in 1803, Jefferson asked Congress for an appropriation of $2,500 to fund a small expedition to explore the Missouri River and to search for a river flowing to the Pacific. He believed that cheap land was a key to American freedom and economic independence from the Old World. He chose Meriwether Lewis, his private secretary, and William Clark, a frontiersman, to head the expedition. He told them: "The object of your mission is single, the direct water communication from sea to sea."

The Lewis and Clark Expedition was to gather information about the flow of rivers, natural resources, climate, and geology. The president was interested in the potential for future commerce, and as a scientist, he was interested in learning more about the land, climate, and history west of the Missouri River. He sent a message to the powerful Osage tribe, who lived south of the Missouri River: "You have furs and pelts which we want, and we have clothes and other useful things which you want. Let us employ ourselves then in mutually accommodating each other." He did not inform Congress of this assignment. Lewis and Clark were aided in their expedition by a Shoshone Indian named Sacajawea, who was an expert in locating edible wild plants. After a two-year journey, Lewis and Clark brought back maps and other information that opened the West to further exploration. The assignment of these two courageous and intelligent explorers to the expedition is one of Jefferson's greatest achievements.

Meriwether Lewis (right) and William Clark (bottom) led an expedition through the newly acquired Louisiana Territory in 1803. *(Courtesy of the Library of Congress)*

That same year, the Philadelphia *Aurora* published an article reporting that Jefferson lived as husband and wife with a mulatto slave named Sally Hemings. The report went on to say that Jefferson had fathered several children by Hemings. According to reporter James Callendar, (the same reporter whom Jefferson had hired to write disparaging stories about Alexander Hamilton) Jefferson had seduced Sally in France, where she became pregnant. Callendar said that Sally remained Jefferson's mistress even while he was president. Jefferson refused to reply to the charges, perhaps because the situation was even more delicate than Callendar knew. Sally Hemings was the child of Jefferson's father-in-law, making her a half-sister to Jefferson's late wife, Martha.

Jefferson asked his daughters to join him in Washington for an extended visit, hoping that his opponents would stop the talk of scandal if his daughters were in the capital. Also, the stress and depression were threatening to overpower him. Perhaps the presence of the two people he loved the most would help to ease his emotional problems. Although both his daughters were busy with their growing families, they did come to visit him in Washington for six weeks.

By 1804, every state north of Maryland had abolished slavery. But in the South, especially in Virginia, the Carolinas, and Georgia, the invention of the cotton gin doomed the possibility of abolition. The gin sped up the time-consuming task of removing seeds from the cotton, and now plantation owners could grow and process much more cotton than before. They needed even more slaves to do the plowing, planting, and preparation for market.

In 1804, Republicans re-nominated Jefferson for president. The Federalist candidate was Charles C. Pinckney. Just as Jefferson had done, the nominating committee completely ignored Burr, instead nominating George Clinton, governor of New York, for vice president. Jefferson's election seemed certain. The Republican party had gained strength since his inauguration. Almost half the thirty-two Senators and 106 Representatives were Republican. Although this was not formally acknowledged at the time, Jefferson was the first president of the United States who was also head of a party. He was popular and remained a voice for freedom and a statesman who represented all the people.

The Jefferson-Clinton ticket won by a landslide. The pleasure of his victory, though, was overshadowed by the death in childbirth of Jefferson's daughter, twenty-four-year-old Polly. Jefferson had her buried near her mother and all the tiny children who had died

George Clinton was elected vice president for Jefferson's second term.
(Courtesy of the Library of Congress)

at Monticello. He despaired that he would never re-cover from grief.

In his inaugural address, Jefferson spoke in his fa-miliar low voice which few in the audience could hear. He enumerated what he called the successes of his first term—living up to his campaign promises, elimination of waste in government, freedom from internal taxes, and adherence to the Constitution. He also mentioned a potentially explosive problem—Native Americans. He had spoken to the native tribes of Miamis, Powtewatmies, and Weeauks early in 1802, saying, "Peace, brothers, is better than war." He proposed that they be taught more of white people's ways and urged Native Americans to consider agriculture as a respectable and even uplifting occupation. This may have sounded like a good idea to white citizens, but it ignored the fact that many Native Americans were nomadic and that an agrarian lifestyle went against their heritage and tradition.

Foreign policy disputes occupied much of Jefferson's second term in office. Except for the good news that Tripoli signed a favorable treaty with the United States, shipping and other international affairs seemed bleak. Spain challenged the boundaries defined in the Louisi-ana Purchase, and relations with Spain deteriorated as Jefferson attempted to negotiate a treaty concerning the land in Florida and the western boundaries of the frontier. On the eastern coast of the United States, the British seized American ships they claimed were in violation of international shipping laws. In return,

Jefferson authorized the building of gunboats and war-ships.

Relations continued to fester as Jefferson tried to work out a satisfactory trade agreement with Britain. Frustrated by his lack of success, Jefferson persuaded Congress to vote to ban certain British goods in the near future. He hoped that the threat would convince the British to agree to a trade treaty. The threat did not work, and the law went into effect in November. Although unhappy merchants bombarded Jefferson with protests because the new law would restrict their business, the federal government tried to enforce the act with prosecutions, seizures, and penalties. After five weeks of demonstrations and non-compliance, Jefferson suspended the ban until reconsideration in the summer of 1807. Again, opponents, and some supporters, accused the president of procrastinating.

In his sixth annual message to Congress in December 1806, Jefferson expressed concern about the Spanish presence in America and promised to try more negotiation before he relied on force to settle the problems. He praised the success of explorers Lewis and Clark. He also asked for congressional approval to set aside monies for public education.

In 1807, a British ship demanded the right to search the U.S. Naval vessel *Chesapeake* as it sailed near the Virginia capes. Before the American commander could answer, the British fired three cannon shots, wounding eighteen and killing three American seamen. Jefferson ordered the British out of American waters and called for Congress to discuss the situation within three months. He was roundly criticized by his opponents for not declaring war on Britain immediately. They repeated the accusation that was becoming too familiar—that Jefferson was a procrastinator. He gave his critics more to complain about when he left for Monticello after pronouncing his decision to wait. As happened more and more frequently, citizens and politicians complained about Jefferson's frequent trips to his home. In his own defense, Jefferson answered that he did a lot of writing at Monticello. A copy of his 1807 schedule shows that he was in Monticello from April 7 to May 16, and from August 1 to October 3.

Jefferson wanted the United States to remain neutral toward the war raging in Europe between Britain and France, and Madison agreed with him. But American ships headed for European ports were often stopped by both the British and the French, each hoping to capture deserters or supplies bound for enemy territory. By 1807, France had seized 500 U.S. ships, and Britain had seized 1,000. Jefferson's dilemma was to preserve American shipping rights while remaining neutral in the conflict. He imposed an embargo against both France and England, hoping it would convince the leaders of these two countries that American trade was far more important to them than the potential threat of American ships aiding the enemy.

Jefferson's plan backfired. The embargo hurt American business more than it hurt Europe by creating an underground economy of smuggling rings and illicit trade beyond the control of customs officials. The worst depression in America since the Revolution followed. To add to Jefferson's problems, American businessmen resented the imposition of regulations, especially from a president who continually preached about the right of citizens to be free of government interference.

The following year, a Republican judge indicted editors of certain Federalist publications for libel against Jefferson. The president, who supported freedom of the press, agreed with the indictment. He declared that any libel of the United States government and its leaders would "sap the foundations of our Constitution of Government [more] than any kind of treason."

During 1806 and 1807, the threat of treason was discovered in someone close to the presidency. Aaron Burr, Jefferson's former vice president, was suspected of being involved in conspiring with the Spanish against America. Jefferson had received several reports that Burr had met secretly with Spanish officials to plan to seize the Louisiana Territory and separate it from the United States. The president had ignored these warnings for a couple of years, but in 1807, feeling heat from U.S. government officials, Jefferson exposed the plot, denounced Burr, and demanded a full investigation. Burr was indicted for treason and charged with plotting with Spain to overthrow the U.S. government. Jefferson was convinced that Burr had been involved in the conspiracy. The defense and the prosecution agreed that plans had been made on Blennerhasset's Island in the Ohio River on December 10, 1806. Because the prosecution was unable to prove that Burr had been present at that particular time, he was acquitted. Jefferson declared that the ruling was politically motivated.

In November, Jefferson gave his eighth, and last, annual message. He assured Congress that he had made errors in the presidency but that they were all due to misunderstanding, not to lack of concern or dedication. He said as he retired from office, "I carry with me the consolation of a firm persuasion that Heaven has in store for our beloved country long ages to come of prosperity and happiness."

Jefferson had refused the pleas of Republicans to run for a third term. In 1808, James Madison won the presidency over the Federalist candidates by 122 to 47 electoral votes. In Jefferson's mind, this election vindicated all he had done for the Republican party.

Chapter Nine

Monticello

Jefferson had accumulated a $30,000 debt while serving as president. He borrowed $8,000 to pay off some of his debts before he left Washington. He had served the public for forty years, ever since his first election to the House of Burgesses, and now he had no pension from any of his service. Emotionally and physically weary, he needed rest and recuperation perhaps even more than he needed money. He hoped that farming would soothe him. He counted it as a blessing that Patsy lived near him with her husband and eight children.

When he retired to Monticello in 1809, Jefferson had plans for another radical renovation of his estate. He spent much of his time away from family hustle and bustle, surrounded by his books, his measuring devices, his polygraph, and his writing materials. He enjoyed carpentry and kept a workbench and tools near his study. He tended to his gardens and groves, planting 250 more varieties of vegetables and 150 more varieties of fruit trees. Always fascinated with machines, he invented a new seed box for sowing, perfected a machine to aid in harvesting hemp, and experimented with different spinning machines.

His greatest joy came from his grandchildren, with whom he spent hours. His house was always filled with grandchildren, nieces, nephews, and the children of friends. Along with these frequent visitors was a steady stream of former colleagues, neighbors, and friends. Young men came too, asking to get help in studies, to receive advice in preparing for a political career, and simply to sit at the feet of a man whom they greatly admired.

Shortly after he retired, Jefferson resumed his correspondence with John Adams. A mutual friend had urged these two legends of the American Revolution to renew the ties that had bound them for so long. When Adams was assured that Jefferson wanted to rekindle the friendship, he said, "I always loved Jefferson, and still love him." When this was relayed to Jefferson, he answered, "This is enough for me." Adams agreed: "You and I ought not to die, before we have explained ourselves to each other." Their correspondence lasted for fourteen years, until neither was physically able to continue. The topics of their letters ranged from discourses on government to remembrances of American history to philosophical statements about Roman and European history. They also included discussion of the pronunciation of ancient Greek, spiritualism, the nature of aristocracy, and their current reading. They continued their

disagreements concern-
ing effective govern-
ment, with Jefferson ar-
guing the importance of
a large educated citi-
zenry and Adams back-
ing a governing aristoc-
racy. On one matter on
which they had strongly
differed in the past, the
two men came closer to
agreement. Jefferson
had become a disciple
of the morals of Chris-
tianity; Adams had em-
braced the attitude of

This bronze bust of Thomas Jefferson, reminiscent of a Roman leader, was made in 1825. *(Courtesy of the Library of Congress)*

Reason encouraged by the Enlightenment. Each man's
personality came across in his letters: Jefferson's letters somewhat resembled essays, while Adams's were
spontaneous and natural.

In early 1814, seventy-one-year-old Jefferson was
invited to become a trustee of a small private school
called Albemarle Academy. This was the impetus for
one of Jefferson's greatest achievements. He planned
to make Albemarle into a fine university, "the most
eminent in the United States," as he wrote.

He drew up plans for a great domed library and
designed a campus with lawns and garden beds. He
recruited faculty, drew up class schedules, and com-

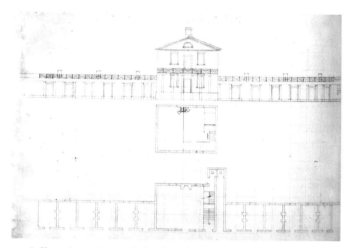

Jefferson's architectural drawings for the University of Virginia.
(Courtesy of the Library of Congress)

piled lists of student rules. Jefferson insisted that students should be free to choose their own courses of study within a framework focusing on the principles of government. He also insisted that the college be open to capable students, whether or not they could afford it. He bragged that the university would be based on freedom of the mind, having no religious affiliation whatsoever. He said that the creation of the University of Virginia in Charlottesville was "the last service I can render my country."

In the early fall of 1814, Jefferson offered his personal library to Congress to replace the volumes burned by the British in the War of 1812. Jefferson's 3,000 books would more than double the number of volumes in the original collection. He called them, "the choicest collection of books in the United States," and asked for any payment Congress deemed appropriate. Federalist representatives argued against acquiring the collection because it included too many books that they considered irreligious and immoral, too many in foreign languages, and too many on "unimportant" topics, such as architecture and cooking. After much debate, a bill was passed to buy the collection. In April, Jefferson sent ten wagon loads of pine boxes full of books to Washington. He received almost $24,000 that he used to pay off debts. Immediately, he began collecting books for a new library. He told John Adams, "I cannot live without books."

At eighty-three, Jefferson suffered more financial difficulties. His son-in-law, Patsy's husband, went bankrupt. Jefferson himself was in dire financial straits, and he decided to hold a lottery to collect money to pay his debts. But the public was aghast to see their hero in such a degrading situation. Instead, they sent contributions so that he was able to give up the lottery.

As the fiftieth anniversary of the signing of the Declaration of Independence approached, Jefferson received many invitations to attend celebrations throughout the country, but he was too old to attend. John Adams was also invited to attend many functions, and he too declined on grounds of poor health.

By the spring of 1826, Jefferson suffered from general

(Courtesy of the Library of Congress)

Thomas Jefferson at age seventy-eight.
(Courtesy of the Library of Congress)

weakness, persistent diarrhea, and a chronic infection of the urinary tract. He depended on large doses of the tranquilizer laudanum and became so frail that he could not get out of bed. On July 2, he said his farewells individually to family members and fell into a coma. At 11:00 p.m. on July 3, he woke from the coma to ask if it was the Fourth of July. Not wanting to disappoint Jefferson, his attendant said yes. The doctor offered a dose of laudanum. Jefferson answered, "No, doctor, nothing more." He fell back to sleep. At 4:00 the next morning, he called for his servant, but he did not speak again. Thomas Jefferson died at 1 p.m. on the afternoon of July 4, 1826, as bells rang and cannons boomed throughout the country in honor of independence and the Declaration of Independence. John Adams died on the same day, shortly after 6 p.m. in the evening.

Jefferson was buried beside his wife the next day in a graveside ceremony. His family found instructions he had written earlier about a monument. He asked for a simple stone with the following inscription:

HERE WAS BURIED
THOMAS JEFFERSON
AUTHOR OF THE DECLARATION OF INDEPENDENCE,
OF THE STATUTE OF VIRGINIA FOR RELIGIOUS
FREEDOM,
AND FATHER OF THE UNIVERSITY OF VIRGINIA.

Timeline

1743—Born at Shadwell in Virginia, April 13.
1760—Attends William and Mary College.
1768—Elected to the House of Burgesses.
1772—Marries Martha Wayles Skelton.
1775—Elected to the Continental Congress.
1776—Drafts Declaration of Independence.
1776—Re-elected to House of Burgesses.
1779—Submits bill for establishing freedom of religion in Virginia.
1779—Elected governor of Virginia.
1782—Wife dies.
1783—Elected delegate to Congress.
1784—Appointed minister to France.
1790—Appointed secretary of state.
1797—Elected vice president.
1800—Elected president.
1809—Retires from presidency.
1814—Establishes University of Virginia.
1826—Dies at Monticello.

Sources

CHAPTER ONE: The Young Jefferson

p. 13, "thrown on a wide world . . ." Willard Randall. *Thomas Jefferson: A Life* (New York: Henry Holt and Company, 1993), 18.

p. 14, "lessons may be formed . . ." Thomas Jefferson. *Writings* (New York: The Library of America, 1984), 742.

CHAPTER TWO: College Years

p. 16, "His manners could never be harsh. . ." Dumas Malone. *Jefferson the President: Second Term* (Little, Brown and Company, 1977), 130.

p. 17, "Which of these kinds . . ." Randall, *A Life,* 43.

p. 17,
"fixed the destinies . . ." Jefferson, *Writings,* 4.

p. 21, "a lawyer without books . . ." Randall, *A Life*, 67.

p. 22, "Descending then to the valley . . ." Ibid., 112.

p. 22, "If this be treason . . ." Ibid., 77.

CHAPTER THREE: Political Beginnings

p. 27, "Parliament has enslaved us!" Natalie S. Bober, *Thomas Jefferson: Man on a Mountain* (New York: Atheneum, 1988), 56.

p. 28, "Our minds were circumscribed . . ." Jefferson, *Writings,* 5.

p. 29, "You have made it my duty . . ." Alf Mapp, Jr., *Thomas Jefferson: A Strange Case of Mistaken Identity* (New York: Madison Books, 1987), 51.

p. 30, "mutual defence against . . ." Gilbert Chinard, *Thomas Jefferson: The Apostle of Americanism* (Boston: Little, Brown, and Company, 1929), 45.

p. 32, "Happy the man who, far away . . ." Randall, *A Life,* 41.

p. 36, "Open your breast, Sire . . ." Mapp, *Strange Case,* 87.

p. 36, "The God who gave us life . . ." Jefferson, *Writings,* 122.

CHAPTER FOUR: Declaration of Independence

p. 37, "Give me liberty . . . "Bober, *Man,* 88.

p. 38, "blows must decide . . ." James W. Davidson and Mark H. Lytle, *The United States: A History of the Republic* (New Jersey: Prentice-Hall, Inc., 1981), 122.

p. 43, "Can any reason be assigned . . ." James T. Adams, *The Living Jefferson* (New York: Charles Scribner's Sons, 1936), 63.

p. 43, "we must drub you soundly . . ." Fawn Brodie, *Thomas Jefferson: An Intimate History* (New York: W.W. Norton & Co., 1974), 111.

p. 44, "Tyranny, like hell, is not . . ." John Jakes, *The Rebels* (New York: Jove Books, 1978), 274.

p. 48, "all men are by nature . . ." Mapp, *Strange Case,* 109.

p. 48, "It is honorable . . ." Henry Steele Commager, *Jefferson, Nationalism, and the Enlightenment* (New York: George Braziller, 1975), xiv.

p. 50, "When in the course . . ." Carl Becker, *The Declaration of Independence* (New York: A.A. Knopf, 1942), 14.

p. 52, "He [the king] had suffered . . ." Randall, *A Life,* 278.

p. 52 "a cruel war against nature itself . . ." Noble E. Cunningham, Jr., *In Pursuit of Reason* (Baton Rouge: Louisiana State University Press, 1987), 47.

p. 54, "We must endeavor to forget . . ." Brodie, *Intimate History*, 122.

p. 54, "The pusillanimous idea . . ." Randall, *A Life*, 276.

CHAPTER FIVE: Governor

p. 62, "private retirement . . ." Randall, *A Life*, 308.

p. 69, "I have retired . . ." Bober, *Man*, 144.

p. 71, "Indeed, I tremble . . ." Randall, *A Life*, 171.

CHAPTER SIX: Federal Appointments

p. 76, "If you love me then . . ." Brodie, *Intimate History*, 171.

p. 76, "Having to my habitual ill health . . ." Ibid., 180.

p. 76, "talks much and does nothing" Randall, *A Life,* 359.

p. 76, "After the year 1800 . . ." Ibid., 363.

p. 76, "The voice of a single individual . . ." Brodie, *Intimate History*, 183.

p. 82, "There is scarcely an evil . . ." Bernard Bailyn, *Faces of Revolution: Personalities and Themes in the Struggle for American Independence* (New York: Alfred Knopf, 1990), 27.

p. 82, "No American should come . . ." Ibid., 28.

p. 82, "it was impossible for anything . . ." Jefferson, *Writings*, 57.

p. 82, "that nation [England] hates us . . ." Randall, *A Life*, 415.

p. 85, "I was much an enemy . . ." Randall, Ibid., 482.

p. 85, "The spirit of resistance . . ." Randall, Ibid., 481.

p. 85, "The tree of liberty . . ." Cunningham, *In Pursuit*, 116.

p. 85, "The gay and thoughtless Paris . . ." Brodie, *Intimate History*, 238.

p. 85, " I observe women and men . . ." Randall, *A Life*, 455.

p. 86, "No society can make . . ." Ibid., 486.

p. 88, "When the door of the carriage . . ." Brodie, *Intimate History*, 248.

p. 91, "came on every day . . ." Randall, *A Life*, 517.

CHAPTER SEVEN: Vice President

p. 94, "to be liberated . . ." Randall, *A Life*, 517.

p. 95, "Jefferson thinks by this step . . ." Merrill Peterson, *Adams and Jefferson: A Revolutionary Dialogue* (Athens: The University of Georgia Press, 1976), 64.

p. 95, "I have returned . . ." Brodie, *Intimate History*, 277.

p. 96, "Architecture is my delight . . ." Bober, *Man,* 227.

p. 96, "I am convinced . . ." David McCullough, *John Adams.* (New York: Simon & Schuster, 2001), 451.

p. 98, "The second office is honorable . . ." Randall, *A Life*, 523.

p. 98, "your administration may be filled . . ." McCullough, *John Adams*, 465.

p. 100, "It gives me great regret . . ." Brodie, *Intimate History*, 307.

p. 100, "It is of immense consequence . . ." Randall, *A Life*, 526.

p. 101, "millions for defense . . ." Ibid., 528.

p. 101, "I am obliged to look . . ." Peterson, *Revolutionary Dialogue*, 74.

p. 101, "We owe gratitude . . ." Adams, *Living Jefferson*, 280.

p. 106, "a mischievous enemy . . ." Brodie, *Intimate History*, 332.

p. 106, "as unprincipled and dangerous . . ." Ibid.

CHAPTER EIGHT: President

p. 107, "If I were to go over . . ." Mapp, *Strange Case*, 396.

p. 108 "Every difference of opinion . . ." Ibid., 398.

p. 108, "peace, commerce and honest friendship . . ." Randall, *A Life,* 548.

p. 114, "drest, or rather *undrest* . . ." Cunningham, *In Pursuit*, 258.

p. 115, "As far as I can judge . . ." Brodie, *Intimate History*, 235.

p. 117, "Another year has come . . . " Ibid., 365.

p. 118, "The object of your mission . . ." Malone, *Second Term*, 183.

p. 118, "You have furs and pelts . . ." Ibid., 185.

p. 122, "Peace, brothers, is better than war." Jefferson, *Writings*, 333.

p. 125, "sap the foundations of our Constitution . . ." Randall, *A Life,* 572.

p. 126, "I carry with me the consolation . . ." Jefferson, *Writings,* 549.

CHAPTER NINE: Back to Monticello

p. 128, "I always loved Jefferson . . ." Peterson, *Revolutionary Dialogue,* 103.

p. 128, "This is enough . . ." Ibid., 111.

p. 128, "You and I ought not to die . . ." Ibid.

p. 129, "the most eminent . . ." Randall, *A Life,* 587.

p. 130, "the last service . . ." Bober, *Man,* 245.

p. 130, "The choicest collection of books . . ." *American Heritage.* August 1958, Vol IX, No. 5, 65.

p. 132, "No, doctor, nothing more." *John Adams,* 646.

Bibliography

Adams, James Truslow. *The Living Jefferson*. New York: Charles Scribner's Sons, 1936.

Bailyn, Bernard. *Faces of Revolution: Personalities and Themes in the Struggle for American Independence*. New York: Alfred Knopf, 1990.

Becker, Carl. *The Declaration of Independence*. New York: A.A. Knopf, 1942.

Bober, Natalie S. *Thomas Jefferson: Man on a Mountain*. New York: Atheneum, 1988.

Boyd, Julius (ed.). *The Papers of Thomas Jefferson, vol. 1-17*. Princeton: Princeton University Press, 1965.

Brodie, Fawn. *Thomas Jefferson: An Intimate History*. New York: W.W. Norton & Co., Inc. 1974.

Chinard, Gilbert.. *Thomas Jefferson: The Apostle of Americanism*. Boston: Little, Brown, and Company, 1929.

Commager, Henry Steele. *Jefferson, Nationalism, and the Enlightenment*. New York: George Braziller, 1975.

Cunningham, Noble.E, Jr. *In Pursuit of Reason*. Baton Rouge: Louisiana State University Press, 1987.

Davidson, James W. and Lyle, Mark H. *The United States: A History of the Republic*. New Jersey: Prentice-Hall, Inc., 1981.

Jakes, John. *The Rebels*. New York: Jove Books, 1978.

Jefferson, Thomas. *The Commonplace Book of Thomas Jefferson.* Baltimore: Johns Hopkins University, 1925.

———. *The Literary Bible of Thomas Jefferson.* New York: Greenwood Press, 1928.

———. *Writings.* New York: The Library of America, 1984.

Jefferson, Thomas (Adrienne Koch and William Peden, eds.). *The Life and Selected Writings of Thomas Jefferson.* New York: The Modern Library, 1944.

Levi, Peter. *Horace: A Life.* New York: Routledge,1998.

Livy. *The Early History of Rome.* New York: Penguin Books, 1960.

Malone, Dumas. *Jefferson the President: Second Term 1805-1809.* Boston: Little, Brown and Company, 1974.

Mapp, Alf F., Jr. *Thomas Jefferson: A Strange Case of Mistaken Identity.* New York: Madison Books, 1987.

McCullough, David. *John Adams.* New York: Simon & Schuster, 2001.

Peterson, Merrill. *Adams and Jefferson: A Revolutionary Dialogue.* Athens: The University of Georgia Press, 1976.

Randall, Willard Sterne. *Thomas Jefferson: A Life.* New York: Henry Holt and Company, 1993.

WEBSITES

Thomas Jefferson Online Resources at the University of Virginia
http://etext.lib.virginia.edu/jefferson/

The Home of Thomas Jefferson
http://www.monticello.org/

Library of Congress site
http://www.loc.gov/exhibits/jefferson/

The Architecture of Thomas Jefferson
http://www.iath.virginia.edu/wilson/home.html

Index